RAMBLING ON

Lost on the Cleveland Way

Paul Amess

For my wife, who is more fun than bubble wrap.

CHAPTER 1
Introduction

I have spent the day trying to find things and generally getting under my wife's feet. All of my camping gear was scattered around the house as well as in the shed. Luckily, everything I do manage to find seems to be in fairly good condition, which is good as I don't particularly want to be spending any money at the moment. The reason being that I had a car accident recently, nothing bad, but it will still cost a substantial sum to repair. I reminded myself that the main thing is that no one was injured and that the only damage was to a great hunk of metal that can be fixed, and to my foolish pride.

In the shed, I found various sleeping bags, which I dusted off and had a good look at. I narrowed the choice down to two and took them in the house for further examination. By further examination, what I mean is that I found the kitchen weighing scales and weighed each one. This might sound a bit extreme, and indeed my wife sat somewhat bemused as I carefully weighed each item, but all I can say in defence is you try carrying around 18 kilos of stuff on your back every day for a week and then get back to me. One of the sleeping bags definitely felt heavier than the other, and if I could save even just a bit of weight somehow, I was certainly going to do it.

The first bag, a dark grey one, was slightly fatter than a blue one, but it felt a bit lighter. Popping it onto the scales, this was confirmed when the display showed 1.1 kg, compared to 1.4 kg when I weighed the blue one, which made the choice easy. I weighed a few other things, an action which was, incidentally, what made me decide not to take them. As I looked at all of my camping gear spread before me, I could not ignore the irony that I had spent a small fortune to basically live like a homeless person for a while. Oh, well.

I had already made a list of things I intended to take. This was for two reasons. The first was so that I could make sure I did actually have everything I needed when it came to packing, and the second was so that I could go through that list a couple of times and try to weed out items that were not particularly essential. I didn't remove much but figured I would not need a lighter as it was very unlikely that we would have a fire one night, and I did remove a couple of packets of food, as there would be plenty of opportunities to buy it as we went along. I have to admit it was a pretty dumb idea to take a small Bluetooth USB keyboard, but at the time I thought it was the smart thing to do. Every night when we had stopped walking, I would sit and do a quick write up of that day, capturing it while it was fresh in my mind. The intention was good, but like I said, it was, in retrospect, a dumb idea.

I did pack things like instant noodles and breakfast bars, as well as a bit of chocolate and some nuts and raisin mix. I nearly didn't get any of this, however. I had been to a supermarket the previous night which I am not going to name, but I can say that I have less reasons to go there now. I was served by perhaps the rudest person I have ever encountered in my life, and that is saying something, trust me. I must point out that I know several people who work in this exact shop, so we should not tar everyone with the same brush, so with that in mind, I will try to cut a long story short. Someone had at some point given us a gift card which had sat in a draw languishing unused and heading speedily towards its expiry date, as these things tend to do. I thought this shopping trip the ideal opportunity to finally make use of it and took it with me to use as part payment. I stood happily at the till while the operator, let's call her Jezebel, gossiped away with the customer in front of me for what seemed like forever. I did not bite, however, as I was not in any way in a hurry that night, being as I was, an under-employed writer of little repute.

I knew I was in trouble, though, as soon as she began serving me. My feeble 'hello' was met with what I can only describe as a grunt. She scanned all of my items, and I presented said voucher, which she inspected disparagingly assuming it to be a counterfeit or something, and then attempted to scan it, but there was no satisfying bleep in response. She tried it a couple of times but then said bluntly that it was not working, so I asked her to do it again, at which point she heaved a big sigh and gave me a look that said something unprintable. When I suggested that she could perhaps try to key in the number instead of scanning, it was as if I had asked her to murder a little bunny rabbit, and she merely repeated that the voucher was invalid, which I knew was not so.

We were clearly at a stalemate. I only had enough money to pay the difference so had no choice but to use the voucher, so suggested that Jezebel get a different scanning gun, to which she replied that there was nothing wrong with her gun. She must have seen my eyebrows raise, and in a fit of a temper, she scanned the voucher once more, and hey presto, it worked. It was the gun. She was already apologizing to the person in the queue after me for this moron that had dared to use a voucher and twittering that it was not her gun, it was the way I held the voucher, or swamp gas, or something. I don't normally complain to companies about rude service, this is England after all, but there was no way I was going to pass up this opportunity, oh no. As soon as I got home, I contacted their customer services, ha, is that what they call it, and told them that in future, they can go whistle for my £9.20 and that from now on I was a Tesco man. Or an Asda man. Or anything but their man anyway. So be warned all you businesses out there, as we men get older, we get grumpier, so you had better watch out. You have been warned, and we take no prisoners, especially when you ignore my complaint.

Anyway, by the time I had finished packing and sorting, and my blood pressure had gone back down to something like normal, I had my backpack down to 17 kg, which was a small saving but as they say, every little helps. I tried the pack on, adjusted the straps for the best fit, and it was fine, which meant only one thing. We were ready to go.

Since our little wander across England a while back, I had been itching to get out and about again, get some fresh air, stretch my legs, and all that. The elephant in the room, however, was the dreaded Coronavirus, or Covid-19, or whatever you want to call it. As we all know, this brought life as we know it to a complete standstill and for a while ruled out anything other than 60 minutes of freedom, per person, per day.

I had always enjoyed walking but had never imagined in my life that my enjoyment of it would ever be rationed by the government, which is basically what happened. I am not necessarily complaining, as we have to put these things into perspective, which is that people were dying. Plus, it could have been worse. If we had lived in Spain, for instance, the police were quite likely to snatch you off the street and bundle you into the back of a car if you dared venture out for a jog at the wrong time of day in breach of local regulations.

An hour was definitely not enough, however, and as restrictions in the UK began to be lifted, my thoughts returned to a nice long walk. I had a chat with my good friend Rob, who had accompanied me on the 54 Degrees Walk across England, and he said he was up for it too. Chris, however, would be unable to come due to work commitments, so it would be just the two of us.

No date was set, however, as the situation still seemed to be somewhat erratic, with talk of fresh lockdowns somewhere down the road, plus we were due to be going on holiday to the south of France in August. When it became apparent that international travel would not be possible, we decided to make use of the week where we had intended to travel to France and to go for another wander.

Rob somehow managed to use a bit of reverse psychology trickery upon his wife, and it was subsequently her who suggested to my wife that we disappear for a week and give them some peace and quiet. I guess when you have been locked up with someone for four months, this becomes wholly possible and probably quite desirable. So, it was decided that during the last week of August, we would walk the Cleveland Way, starting in Helmsley and finishing in Filey, a journey or around 109 miles according to the guidebook. There was only one catch, my wife said, and that was to get in touch with her daily, just in case, and I assured her that I would. I reminded her that I'm not a natural outdoorsman, so if I did go missing, say for three days, then she must simply assume that I had been dead for at least two of them. I didn't want her worrying, you see. I think, in retrospect, she just wanted to know when she might be able to claim on my insurance.

It looked like an interesting route, which was sort of naturally split into two wholly distinctive sections. The first part followed the edge of the North Yorkshire Moors more or less sticking to the high ground. An initial saunter west towards Sutton Bank and the Kilburn White Horse would then see a right turn take you north to Osmotherley. After this, east became the general direction, skirting the northern edge of the hills before turning north for a run to Saltburn on the coast of the North Sea. At this point, the character of the walk would change completely, and you would from now on be hugging the dramatic Yorkshire coast. Turning more or less south-east for the rest of the walk, the delightful villages of Staithes and Runswick Bay would lead you into Whitby and all that it offers. Robin Hoods Bay and Ravenscar would then guide you into Scarborough before a final run to Filey Brigg would bring you to the end of the trail.

We figured we would spend around a week walking the route, and as we did not want to stop in any hotels along the way, we would wild camp. Having had some experience of this before, we knew that although it was technically illegal in England, there probably would not be any problems in finding suitable places. Camping like this would serve two purposes, the first one being that neither of us had great amounts of cash to spend on hotels or guest houses, as we had both been furloughed from our jobs to one extent or another. Secondly, we didn't particularly want to be going to any places that would involve extensive human contact, as there was certainly still transmission of the virus happening every day, with hot-spots popping up seemingly randomly around the country. It is important to say that at this point all restrictions on travel had been lifted, and we saw this as an opportunity to escape for a bit of freedom before the next inevitable lockdown came, probably sometime in the autumn. This was also going to be a proper camping trip, not like some of our previous efforts, which could more accurately be described as getting drunk in the woods. My wife had been camping with us on one or two occasions, though she was not a great fan, and preferred her home comforts. When I once said that camping was a tradition in my family, she replied that it had been a tradition in everyone's family until someone invented the house, so I figured she was never going to be converted.

Anyway, it would be an adventure, despite my track record with camping. My first camping trip had been with my school, many moons ago somewhere around Easter, so it wasn't exactly summer. It was at one of those outdoor activity centres, and the school were too frugal to pay for the cabins, so we had leaky old tents instead. It rained for two days, was sunny but cold on the third, and snowed on the last day, and I think we all came home with the flu, so I reckoned that no camping trip could ever be as bad as that.

So, it was with this intention in mind that we did a final check of our bags, said goodbye to our respective kids, who either grunted in response, not wanting to divert their attention from their Xboxes or whatever, or ignored us completely, and headed off out and into the woods and the fields of Yorkshire. They will miss me, I thought, as soon as the internet goes down, they will miss me.

CHAPTER 2
Helmsley to Osmotherley (nearly)

The ladies dropped us off in Helmsley at around 10 am on a Saturday morning towards the end of August 2020. Their willingness to take us led me to suspect that they wanted to be rid of us following what had been, by any account and as we all know well, a very odd year. Lockdown had ensured that many people had spent more time with their loved ones such as their husband or wife, their children or their parents, or in some especially cruel examples, their in-laws, than they had in many years or perhaps even decades. I had heard it said that there will, in around nine months following lockdown, be either a baby-boom or a spike in divorce cases, or more probably a combination of both.

The Cleveland Way starts (or ends) in Helmsley, and follows a horseshoe shape around the North Yorkshire Moors National Park, finally finishing at Filey. Most people do the walk in a clockwise direction, and we were going to go with the flow on this one. The plan today was to go east around ten miles, to Sutton Bank, where we would make a quick diversion to see the Kilburn White Horse, before heading north towards Osmotherley, where we would enjoy the best fish and chips in the north of England apparently, before falling asleep in an idyllic campsite somewhere in the beautiful woods. It all sounded perfect at the planning stage, but I think at the back of my mind, there was a slight awareness that things don't always go according to plan.

Anyway, Helmsley is a very nice town; the National Park Authority has its headquarters here, and I'm told that Gareth Southgate once stayed at The Feathers Hotel, as did Tony Robinson. This is also where Boris Johnson started his political career, apparently, so you may or may not want to thank the place for that, depending on which political party is your favourite flavour. There is also a company based here called Ample Bosom, which sells bras, specializing in plus sizes apparently, which is good to know for us ageing men. So, there you go.

Anyway, as we got out of the car, the rain started more or less immediately. I had not really checked the weather forecast other than having a quick glance, which had suggested the occasional shower. Parking next to the Royal Oak, we donned our wet gear and plodded on to the market place, where a cross marked the official start of the Cleveland Way. We figured that parking the car there would mean that it would still be there later on, as the streets around here can sometimes be dangerous. Just around the corner, a small home on a little road called Ryegate is a prime example, in fact, I think this particular house might actually be cursed and is quite possibly the most unlucky house in Yorkshire.

Way back in 1971, a bus heading from Stokesley came over the hump-back bridge that crosses the River Rye here, just before Ryegate, at considerable speed. It quickly lost control, then managed to hit a car before finally smashing into the house on the corner, killing 10 people including two in the car. The bus had defective brakes, tyres and springs as well as six loose nuts on one of the back wheels, and one loose nut behind the steering wheel presumably, which was standard safety protocol in the 1970s if I remember rightly. All was put right by the tough British criminal justice system though, who fined the owner of the bus £200. Bizarrely, a BBC film crew that had travelled from Leeds to film the scene of this accident were themselves involved in an accident the next day. Rather than driving the 50-odd mile journey, for some reason, probably because they could put it on expenses, they chose to fly. In retrospect, this was not their best decision ever, as their plane crashed while attempting to take off from nearby Sutton Bank, about 10 miles further along on our journey. The pilot clipped a dry-stone wall, aborted the take-off attempt and put the plane back down again, and when it had almost stopped, it unceremoniously nosed over until it was upside down.

In 1976, presumably just after the house had been nicely rebuilt and re-decorated with some of the finest trippy wallpaper of the time, a car travelling in exactly the same direction lost control, bounced over the bridge and went straight into the recently renovated living room, instantly remodelling the place with a more al fresco feel. The BBC chose to stay away this time, just in case, and the occupants of the car jumped out and ran away too. Unbelievably, history repeated itself once again in 2011. Poor Eveline Broad was happily snoozing away one night, when, guess what, a car ran out of control, bounced over the bridge, and went straight into the living room once again. I can just imagine her dragging herself out of bed and thinking to herself *I'm moving*. I reckon this would be a really cheap house to buy, though, and whoever has the misfortune to live there would do well to invest in, say, a tank to park out front, or maybe some of those anti-terrorist bollards that they have in London. If you want to see this house, finding it is easy. It's the one with all the patchy brickwork.

Anyway, once in the market place, we decided to get the obligatory pre-walk photo. For this, we headed over to the impressive monument to Lord Feversham and stood dripping in the drizzle as the ladies proceeded to take far too many pictures of us than was required. I'm sure they just wanted to make us stand there for the sake of it, for a laugh, perhaps. Incidentally, Feversham was apparently an all-round nice guy, which is great for him, but not great for an aspiring writer trying to dig up dirt or fun facts on someone, so we shall move on.

    Photos taken, and with a quick goodbye kiss to my wife, and a hug to my youngest Max, we ventured back past the pub, catching a quick glimpse of the impressive castle, before turning left onto a road aptly named Cleveland Way, which reassured us that we were going in the right direction, at this early stage anyway. With the rain now coming down fairly heavily, it was a case of heads down as we trudged past the castle car park to join the path out of the town. There is still a fair bit of the castle left, but someone had told me that the town's people had pulled most of the walls down, which resulted in some very nice houses going up. There was also a bench here which appeared to be there to mark another possible starting point of this walk, but we decided to miss this photo opportunity because of the now relentless rain. On it was a carving of a huge acorn, a smaller version of which would become very familiar to us over the next few days, and at times would be a sight for sore eyes when we thought we might be lost. A soggy dog walker gave us a cheery good morning and suggested that we had perhaps picked the wrong day to begin a walk of 109 miles or so, before she promptly went home to her nice centrally heated house, no doubt to have a lovely hot cup of Yorkshire tea. I grimaced at her with my most evil face, which probably made me look like I was sucking helium.

Almost immediately, the path became vertically challenged, and we began a steep ascent of what looked like a long hill disappearing into the drizzle ahead. The problem with wearing waterproofs quickly became apparent as I started to sweat while trying to keep up with Rob. He was immediately ahead of me by a considerable distance, despite his pack weighing a lot more than mine. When I had weighed mine the previous day, I had forgotten to put the water in it. It now contained 3 litres of water so would therefore add another 3 kg of unwanted, but essential weight that would ultimately be dispersed through my knees for the next week or so. I found it ironic, though, that we had to carry this around with us when at any point there were thousands of gallons of the stuff, all nice and fresh and clean, falling all around us in every direction.

Under normal circumstances, we would usually carry a bit less, but these were no normal circumstances. The pandemic had made many people wary, and quite rightly so, of answering their door to strangers asking for water and proffering various bottles and pouches into their hands along with any potential traces of the virus that they carried. We had never had a problem in obtaining water from complete strangers, usually just with an unsolicited knock on a door. On this walk at this time though, we were going to have to exercise more caution than usual, not just because people might be reluctant to answer their doors, but also because we didn't want to get the lurgy and die.

At the top of the hill, somewhat out of breath and by now wet through with sweat to the point that I might as well have probably not bothered with waterproofs, the path turned left towards a small wood and at least some shelter from the worst of the rain. A further right turn saw us edge along the side of the wood, bordering farmlands to our right, where we met an elderly gentleman who was making his way along the path at a snail's pace, picking up litter. He had a hi-vis jacket on and a hat similar to my own, which I always find invaluable come rain or shine. There is not much of a worse feeling than that of rain trickling down the back of your neck, or perhaps even the sting of sunburn in the same place. This is subjective, of course, I am sure there are many worse feelings, such as being eaten alive by a polar bear, but you know what I mean.

We stopped to talk to him, and he told us that the paths had been much messier during the lockdown, presumably because of the higher number of people using them. He also said that many of the people out walking were not the sort that would normally enjoy the countryside, hence the littering. I think I understood what he meant, as the disused railway line near to my home, which led across the beautiful countryside towards Hornsea, had been very busy with people making the most of their hour a day. He was doing an excellent job today, however; the path was probably the cleanest it had been in a long time.

We carried on, the skies still dumping on us relentlessly, and came to a sharp downhill section. At the bottom, facing an equal uphill section, we paused momentarily before tackling the precarious and slippery path that awaited us. The pace slowed somewhat as our heart rates increased accordingly. By the time we got to the top, we were both done for. Rob found a good way to rest, placing the weight of his backpack on a section of fence. I attempted the same trick, hoping to take the weight off my back, but found that the fence was suited to someone of Rob's height as opposed to a shortie such as myself. Luckily, though, I found a little rock a few feet away and used it as a platform to artificially increase my height and managed to rest my pack on the fence after all.

I suggested to Rob that perhaps we had made a big mistake and should immediately and eternally decamp back down to the town, specifically to the Royal Oak, which should by now be open and serving a decent breakfast if nothing else, but he just laughed. The persistent and prolonged precipitation around us had now become a deluge, and I mused that perhaps we had by now become as wet as it was possible to get, so we decided to tramp on through the puddles regardless. I did have a slight issue when we started walking again, in that I seemed to have managed to hang myself onto the fence a bit like a coat hung on a coat hook, and Rob had to lift my bag so that I could escape.

We had now been going for less than an hour, and I think the only part of me that was still dry was my feet, a revelation which kind of surprised me. Usually, my feet were the first part of me to become sodden, which was down to the fact that I had never owned what I would call a decent pair of hiking shoes. But I had recently, perhaps a bit too recently, purchased a nice pair of Merrell walking shoes, which although they were doing a good job of resisting the surrounding floodwaters, were perhaps not quite as worn in as I would like them to be. I could feel one of my toes rubbing, which was bad news after just a few minutes walking, and which hinted at a blister forming already, which was not a great start.

We came out of the trees and walked past a nice house which looked like a gatehouse to Duncombe Park, after which we found ourselves back in the woods and once again losing elevation. Nearby, if you have a minute, are the caves of Windypits. I don't know about you, but the big kid in me always feels compelled to explore any caves I come across. This is usually done in the hope of finding some cool stuff, treasure maybe, or abandoned booty, or even a body, even though deep down I know this is never going to happen. Someone did find something in Windypits though, human remains, and after examination, it turned out that at least one of them had been scalped. Yikes.

Emerging on a country road which had temporarily turned into a stream, we rounded a bend to the right and came to Rievaulx Bridge, where we stopped for a rest. Rievaulx Abbey, a lovely ruined Cistercian abbey set in the lush woodlands of the Rye Valley, is just around the corner, and for a minute, I was tempted by the café, until I remembered that they sold various kinds of Gin. While this might be a good thing, it might distract me a bit and mean the end of the day's walking, so I decided to give it a miss. If you have never been to Rievaulx though, you really should go. The ruins are ace, and it is a really good place for a game of hide and seek. My kids were lost for ages, and I got loads of peace and quiet.

The weight of our heavy backpacks was quickly getting to us, and I found myself having doubts as to whether I could carry this for over a hundred miles, so I came up with a cunning plan. I decided to eat as much of the contents as quickly as possible, and by this I meant the food mainly of course. My wife had very kindly made me a packed lunch, which I had somehow managed to squeeze into the top of my rucksack despite it being full, and that was going to be the first to go.

As I took my sandwiches out now, I found out that they were more 2 dimensional than they presumably were when they had been made, but this did not affect the taste. The pork pies came out too, which I shared with Rob, again with the secret aim to lighten my load as much as possible. I figured if we ate through my food first, I might not end up with a broken back. Unfortunately, Rob rumbled me straight away, figuring out my ruse completely and entirely. I shamelessly admitted my guilty intent, though noted that he still ate the pies.

    At this point, the rain had ceased, at least for the time being, and the gentleman who had been clearing the litter caught us up. His identity badge described him as a voluntary ranger and named him as Martin. He was from York, which was less than thirty miles away, and he said he did this sort of thing all the time, combining his hobby of walking with a useful public service, a commendable thing to do if ever there was one. He told us about some of the walks he had done over the years, and we told him about ours before he continued along on his way. We bade him farewell and said we would catch him up in a while, although we never did. I love people like this guy. Nobody has asked him to do it, and he gets no benefit from it other than seeing the countryside a bit tidier, he literally just does it because he can, and makes no attempt to go on and on about it on social media like so many people nowadays who have seen a bandwagon and jumped right on top of it. If everyone was like him, and just got on and did stuff rather than narcissistic preaching and virtue signalling, the world would be a much better place. Sadly, many people are more interested in getting likes, or they want to be seen as woke, than to actually do something that might really make a difference, albeit a small one.

As we packed up to move on, the rain showed signs of starting again, so we put our wet gear back on and headed off. Leaving our picnic site, we got a full glimpse of the little cottage that sat next to the bridge, which was stunningly beautiful. It had hanging baskets full of vividly colourful flowers and a perfectly manicured garden. The garden reminded me of my mum's, which was also always really well-kempt until that is my kids arrived with a football, usually promptly and invariably going straight into her azaleas knocking them for six, though she never seemed to mind.

The road meandered slowly uphill for a mile or so until we turned right to join a track after crossing a stream on some stepping stones. It wasn't immediately obvious which way the path went. Until now, there had been clearly visible signs for the route, but it looked as if some major earthworks were underway at this point, with the giveaway being the scarred earth and the several bright yellow bulldozer type machines parked nearby. A couple of bridges took the path up into the hills, which is nearly the way we went until we decided to stick to the flat track that went into the woods instead. This turned out to be a good choice despite the lack of signposts, as it was, in fact, the correct way.

Rounding a corner, someone had built a small, but quaint log cabin in a long glade, which would be an ideal camping spot had it been ten or so miles further on, but not at this early stage. Just after this, the path turned right, heading directly up a hill, which I renamed Coronary Hill, naming it after that which it nearly gave me. It seemed incredibly steep and seemed to go on forever, and was very slippery underfoot. Eventually passing a gate at the top, we came back out into open fields, where we followed a long track west. Although not as steep, it was still hard work, so the going was slow. Hundreds of grouse dotted our path along here, making their funny little calls as we got too close. Some seemed to be travelling with us, unwilling to turn right or left into the fields, and must have walked a good mile or so in our company. I imagined that they would taste very nice, and wondered what colour wine would go best with them.

We finally arrived in the village of Cold Kirby and quickly took advantage of a bench, using it to balance our rucksacks as we carefully removed them from our aching backs. Once plonked on the bench, we sat in silence while we both enjoyed a chocolate bar which would hopefully provide some much-needed energy. We didn't stop for long as we wanted to keep up a good pace, and besides, the weather was still very threatening. We had figured that just a quick five- or ten-minute break every now and then would give us sufficient rest to refresh us for the next hour or so. Even keeping our backpacks on but resting their weight on something other than our backs helped considerably. I stood up to stretch my calf muscles momentarily and found the village notice board, upon which someone had pinned a rather nice wristwatch that had been found in the village at some point, and I reflected that in many places, this would have been stolen. Looking around, there was little in the village other than the church, St. Michael's, but there were some quite nice houses.

Two sweet old ladies arrived and got into an incredibly small car, and the driver promptly, and perfectly might I say, executed a 12-point turn in what was, admittedly, a narrow sort of road, being only around 40 feet wide, bless her. Still, it entertained us for a moment. The height of excitement arrived when she came dangerously close to hitting a wheelie bin that someone had left out, missing it by a whisker despite her reversing sensor bleeping continually for most of the action.

With backpacks now adorning ourselves once again, we carried on, with the next stop being Sutton Bank and the Kilburn White Horse. The road meandered through fields, quickly becoming a muddy track, emerging at what looked like some kind of small-scale racecourse for horses. It turns out that horse racing and everything that is associated with it goes way back into history around here. As far back as 1715, the Royal Gold Cup was competed for up here, the reason being that the altitude meant that the soil never really dried out, so was probably safer for the horses than many other locations were. This history of horses and racing around here is probably a part of the inspiration for the Kilburn White Horse carved on the hillside nearby. The soil was certainly not dried out today, as we splodged along dodging the puddles. The track took us right through the middle of the farmstead before we turned off and up a steep hill to the road at the top that led to Sutton Bank. Here we passed an old and very large Georgian house which was sadly boarded up, which seemed a real shame. When my lottery win comes in, I thought to myself, that will be mine. But then I remembered about a grisly murder around here and thought perhaps not.

Less than a mile to the east of here lies the site of an enduring and as yet unsolved mystery. In 1981, police found the remains of a woman hidden under a bush, which became known as the nude in the nettles, though it is sometimes called the Sutton Bank Body. The police had received an anonymous tip-off over the phone from a well-spoken gentleman, who strangely claimed that he could not give his details for reasons of national security. Police believed she was murdered, but have never released further details as to why they believe this, and the body had lain there for at least a couple of years.

They initially suspected her to be an escaped inmate from Askham Grange Prison, but after an appeal, they received confirmation that this particular individual inmate was still alive and well after all, and possibly living in Ireland, which is from where she had sent in copies of her fingerprints and her signature. Over the years, the police used various forensic methods to build up quite a detailed picture of the woman, including creating a wax-head lookalike and figuring out that she had given birth at some point. They estimated that she was 35-40 years old and was around 5'4" tall. In 2012, they exhumed her body and completed a full DNA profile which still failed to lead to a match, but did rule out some other possibilities. For now, though, the mystery persists, and it is sad to think that somewhere out there, her children have no idea what happened to their mum.

Sutton Bank is notorious for something else too, and that is for being one of the steepest roads in the country. We could already hear the whine and roar of engines big and small, which all seemed to be either struggling to make it to the top or trying to avoid careering out of control on the steep descent. Crossing the road, we joined a long path towards the bank, which was hemmed in by hedges on both sides, before finally stopping abruptly right at the edge of the steep hill that is Sutton Bank itself. The contrast was immediate and amazing. From having no view whatsoever other than leaf on either side, we could now see for many miles primarily to the west. Looking at the road below us which disappeared into the trees, I'm sure I saw a pile of smashed-up cars at the bottom.

Benches were plentiful, and luckily the first one we saw was empty, so we sat ourselves down and consumed the view. It was a very clear day, and I was amazed to find that I could see the geodesic domes of RAF Menwith Hill, some 25 miles away and, incredibly, one of the hills that makes up Yorkshire's three peaks way off in the Pennines, specifically Whernside, which was almost 50 miles away. This just goes to show how lucky we were for the weather to have cleared up at this point of the walk, some 10 miles from Helmsley. After a brief rest, we got our gear and continued south to see the horse itself. Although I had seen this before and knew that going to see it today would involve a seemingly pointless 3-mile round trip to continue the walk proper, I didn't want to miss any of the route.

The path hugged the edge of the hill on our right, and to our left was an airfield housing the Yorkshire Gliding Club. This site has been used for over one hundred years ever since a nutter called Erik Addyman threw himself off a cliff here in his home-made glider in 1911, which must have taken some serious guts or a couple of bottles of scotch, or possibly both. Erik was said to be keen to fly, and once said that he would give his right arm to be able to do it. Amazingly, Erik didn't die, not that day anyway. As the club developed, they began to use what was essentially a giant elastic band to launch gliders, but at some point, they bought an old Rolls-Royce, took the wheels off, and used that as a winch to drag the craft up into the air. Erik continued his exploits but was seriously injured a few years later in an accident that broke both of his legs and, ironically, resulted in the amputation of a part of his right arm. This is why I don't like gliders. My motto is that if it has to have wings, then it has to have an engine. A recent string of incidents only underlines my feelings on this. Between 2004 and 2006, a series of accidents here resulted in the deaths of four pilots, with one incident seeing two gliders colliding and the debris falling on the main road below the bank. I will stick to walking, thank you very much.

After what seemed like considerably longer than a mile and a half, we finally got to the horse itself. I was under no illusions and realized that this would not be the best vantage point from which to view the old nag. To get a proper view, you would have to either go back to the gliding club, blag yourself a free flight, and pray for the best, or take a very long and steep walk down Sutton Bank to the lower car park, which is where I last saw the horse from. I had no plans to do either of these foolish things. As it was, from up here standing next to the horse's head, almost on its eye, you could have easily walked past without even noticing it was there. This thing is around 300 ft long and well over 200 ft high, so it is next to impossible to appreciate it close up. It is not particularly ancient either, but it was built with inspiration from other such sculptures, particularly the Uffington White Horse in Oxfordshire, which is a bit more abstract but still clearly identifiable as a horse and is considerably more ancient.

There are two people possibly responsible for this horse with the story being a little murky. One account tells of a local schoolmaster called John Hodgson having built it with the labour of some of his pupils, something that would probably be banned nowadays under child labour laws. Another account tells of how a man called Thomas Taylor, after having visited the Uffington horse, had it built here with the help of dozens of men. I am not sure why they chose a horse, other than for the already mentioned history of horse racing in this area, which seems likely but it must be said is only a theory. In the lower car park, there is a gravestone like plaque that I read on my last visit. It states that the horse was 'cut on the initiative of Thomas Taylor', so it's quite possible that both men were involved. What is fairly certain is that it was built in 1857 and is quite hard to maintain and is the most northerly of all of the chalk figures in the British Isles. It can be seen from as far away as Leeds and even Alkborough in North Lincolnshire, so there you go, and during World War Two, the powers that be had the horse covered up so that those resourceful Germans could not use it as a navigation aid.

If Taylor did get his inspiration from a visit to Uffington, then we should be thankful that he never found himself at Cerne Abbas, where a giant figure of a man with an enormous erect penis sports the side of a hill. I've got no problem with this as such, but it is important to point out that while the Cerne Abbas giant has often been the victim of a practical joke, the Kilburn White Horse has not. The giant has, at various times, been decked out with a pair of jeans, been made to wear a giant condom, sported a grass moustache for *Movember*, and, perhaps most worrying of all, seen his 40 ft penis turn purple, which surely required a lot of paint and a visit to the doctor? Having had a good look at the Kilburn horse on my last visit, I can only deduce that it must be a girl horse, as there was definitely no sign of a penis.

Anyway, enough of all of this horsing around. We turned north and cantered on back towards the visitor centre, where we stopped for lunch. We were still looking west over Sutton Bank and could see individual storms raging far away in the valley below. There was one small village that seemed to have been specifically targeted by the rain that day as it had been smothered in the stuff for over an hour now, whereas all of the other rain showers had gradually moved across the countryside. As I ate my lunch, a piece of wrapping blew away, and I found myself running to retrieve it, which I could have done without after four or five hours of walking. I offered Rob more food to further lighten my load, and he did the same, giving me a very nice pulled-pork roll, which I had not tried before but can highly recommend. The section of path near the horse had been comparatively busy, but we now ate all alone, so I figured most people just wander from their car to the horse and back, which was fine by me.

As my mind wandered, I noticed Rob pull out an apple and begin to eat it. This might sound normal, but he left the sticker on, which went down with the first bite. Of course, being the good mate that I am, I didn't tell him until I observed his adam's apple perform what was quite an impressive gulp, signifying the start of the sticker's journey through his digestive system and the obvious conclusion this implied. Annoyingly, when I did inform him, which I may have done in a bit of a smug manner, he told me, also in a bit of a smug manner, that all stickers on food have to be edible due to EU rule number 69 or something like that, which I honestly never knew. Even the glue, he added.

Enjoying the view immensely, I told Rob that somewhere to the west and far below us was the village of Sutton-under-Whitestonecliffe, which is not really famous for anything other than being the longest place name in England, and the second-longest in the UK, after the much more famous Llanfairpwllgwyn, which is the shortened version of course. I had difficulty typing that, so I am not going to attempt the entire thing as that might tip me into a dyslexic fit. The shortest, by the way, is Og. Seriously. It is a river in Wiltshire. There is also a River O, but technically it is the O Brook, so it doesn't count. If you're not happy with the fact that a river is technically a place and you want a town instead, then you need Ae, pronounced eh, which is up in Scotland somewhere. Neither short nor long, Pity Me, in Durham, is just plain unusual, and once again back to my own neck of the woods is the equally odd Land of Nod, in East Yorkshire. And if you want to know the longest place name in the world, it is 85 letters long and located in New Zealand, but you will have to look it up yourself because I am not even going to try. At this point, I had to give Rob a prod with my stick, as he was clearly falling asleep.

We finished lunch and moved on, but I did not feel any difference in the weight of my pack, so decided to adopt Plan B, which was to drink water vigorously from the water pouch inside it. I was pretty sure that we would get the option to refill at some point and decided to only partially refill it next time, more and more confident that on this little island, we were surely never far from a good soaking.

After a few yards, we came across a memorial to the RAF. It described the loss of a Halifax bomber which crashed here in 1943, as well as an F86 Sabre that crashed in 1954. When I later read up on this, the Halifax bomber had been on a mission to bomb Dortmund on the night of 4/5th May and had only gone into service 12 days before, so it was brand spanking new. The Sabre had crashed probably due to a faulty undercarriage door opening mid-flight, and the pilot's remains, he was called Colin Grabham it is important to note, are still at the crash site having never been fully recovered. Sadly, and disgracefully, souvenir hunters have plagued what is essentially an unmarked grave.

We walked on and crossed the road, continuing through more trees before emerging back on the bank looking west. Here we found a viewpoint with a plaque, describing this as the 'finest view in England', words which are attributed to the famous vet and author James Herriot, so must have some authority, and I'm not inclined to disagree. Looking west over the Vale of York, it surely is a beautiful sight, but whether it really is England's finest, I will leave up to you. I would love to spend the night here, as this is also one of the very few places in the country that are renowned for their dark skies, but we have many miles to do before sunset, so we venture on.

The next treat is Gormire Lake, which comes into view within just a few minutes, making this last half hour of the walk more than worthwhile. The lake is not only beautiful to look at from above, but it is a renowned wild swimming spot with the waters said to be described as warm, though I would take that with a pinch of salt and would strongly encourage someone else jump in to test it, probably Rob. It is variously described as bottomless and full of leeches so do this at your own risk though. It is one of the four largest lakes in Yorkshire, with Malham Tarn, Semerwater and of course, from my neck of the woods, Hornsea Mere, being the other three, and is another relic of the ice-age, but a pretty nice one at that.

Carrying on through the woods, we share a path with cyclists for a while, which then splits off, leaving us walkers all alone. By now, the sun is trying to come out, though the wind is picking up. As we leave the woods, the path follows a wide arc to our right, looking as if it will skirt around the top of the hills. It is now mid-afternoon, and the sun is slowly beginning to dip, though it still remains dry. I have a new gadget on my backpack, which is a small portable solar panel, and Rob plugs his phone into it to charge for a bit. We pass a sign for Boltby but carry on towards our current destination of Osmotherley. Boltby is a tiny place and notable only for one thing – residents have been granted free water in perpetuity, which sounds great, but this was taken to the extreme in 2005 when the whole place was flooded under 6 feet of water.

I have already mentioned that we had heard there is a nice fish and chip shop at Osmotherley, and by now, this has become our main incentive to keep on moving. As we follow the path, the woods clear into the first signs of moorland, abundant with heather and the sounds of startled grouse and pheasants as we disturb them with our approach. Crossing a road, we enter another wood, intriguingly named Sneck Yate, this one very muddy underfoot and evidently popular with mountain bikers. After a quick stop to rest our packs on the fence, we slip and slide along trying to avoid the worst patches that look likely to either bring us down as we walk, or suck our shoes and boots from our feet. Our pace, which had not been particularly roadrunner like anyway, slowed further, but we eventually managed to get to a road at the other end without incident or embarrassment.

The road was much better to walk on, but it was a very steep climb. It did not look like it had much traffic and would probably be impassable at the height of winter. I found myself looking at the floor, fatigue beginning to take its toll when I heard Rob shout something. It could have been anything that he shouted, to be honest, but as I looked up a car was careening down the hill with no apparent intention to stop, despite the old, chubby bloke with the backpack in the middle of the road. I just managed to jump out of the way, and, lesson learned, decided to keep at least one eye on what was in front of me at least some of the time.

Rob overtook me on this hill and disappeared around a bend. When I eventually caught him up, he was sat at a picnic table at Paradise Farm, which was not only a farm but was also a campsite and a café. Unfortunately, it closed at 4pm, which was particularly brutal news as a quick look at my watch told me it was ten minutes past. We took the opportunity for a rest anyway and topped up our water pouches a little. As we sat at the picnic table, a very friendly dog came over to see what he could schnaffle, followed by a dozen or so baby geese, along with their protective parents. They were hoovering up the floor around Rob, which is odd as he hadn't eaten anything so I figured that they must have heard he is generally a messy eater. We took a nice long rest here, and Rob unplugged his phone from the solar panel only to find that rather than charge it, the panel had drained the phone's battery. We reckoned this was due to the poor weather and walking in a direction that did not leave the panel pointing in the optimum direction. This gadget had seemed like a good idea, but the technology clearly has some way to go.

Leaving the farm, we soon joined the Hambleton Road, an old drover's road, which quickly brings you to open moorland that is so typical of the moors. Though this route was not so steep, it was particularly gruelling and soon wore us down. The wind was picking up, and once or twice, the solar panel hanging off my pack whipped up and whacked me on the head. I would have felt a bit foolish had there been anyone around, but as it was, I just left it. There was not a lot to see along this stretch.

We passed through a wood, which was eerily quiet, and then once we came back out into the open, we could just about see down to the village of Over Silton in the valley to the west. I only knew that it was Over Silton because I had previously read about a mischievous hobgoblin that was supposed to have lived there and looked up where the place was. Every night the cheeky chappy would come out and churn the farmer's milk for him in exchange for a slice of bread and butter, which was not a bad price to pay, to be honest. But when the farmer forgot one night, the little guy was never seen again, which I thought was a bit of an over-reaction, to be honest. I mean, everyone forgets stuff every now and then.

Not us though, it is hard to forget what we are doing, as the tiredness and pain were building with every step. At this point, I think we had both just decided to focus on putting one step in front of another. Finally, after what seemed an eternity, we arrived at a cairn that marked the end of this section. There was nowhere to sit, but desperate for a rest, we decided to use it as a chair anyway.

This was, in hindsight, clearly a mistake. First of all, as we sat on the stones, many of them moved, taking us with them. Gravity ensured that all movement was in the downward direction, which then posed a further problem. With large packs on our backs and being at a certain level of exhaustion, we found it more or less impossible to get back up. I have heard that when sheep, or perhaps turtles are turned over the wrong way, they too are unable to right themselves, and therefore, if there is no intervention, they simply die. This is the situation we found ourselves in and would have been comical had we been observers. Being participants, however, we did not find this at all funny. Well, not at the time anyway.

The stones eventually slipped to the point that we could not go any further down, so at this point, I turned myself over and got on my hands and knees. With a great deal of effort, I somehow managed to get up and went on to help Rob do the same. I probably do not need to remind you that he is a giant of a man, and in this instance, he was carrying a giant of a backpack. It may come as no surprise then, that when I held out my hands to pull him up, Rob pulled me back down. He had to turn himself over and try to push himself up on all fours while I took the weight of his backpack. As he got on his legs, he almost went back over, but just managed to retain his balance. I am not sure if anyone was watching from a distance, and I was that tired that I would not have cared, but this would probably have looked like a comedy sketch by the Chuckle Brothers, it has to be said.

It was clear that we were nearly done for. Although we were both keen walkers, the actual amount of time that we spent walking meant that we never reached a peak of fitness as such. When I say peak, what I mean is that we never managed to get to a level where we could consistently knock off 20 miles or more each day. Not recently, anyway. The last time that I could say we had managed this was when we walked the Coast to Coast in 2016. After 4 or 5 days on that, we seemed to walk through whatever physical and mental barriers existed and for the rest of the walk, we just nailed it.

Finally up, and ready to walk, we began the steep descent towards Osmotherley. The going was hard on the calves, and I was very glad I had decided to invest in 2 trekking poles, which I do not normally use. The sky was slowly beginning to darken, and although there was still a generous amount of light left, our slow speed made it borderline as to whether or not we would get down the hill before dark. To compound all of this, it started to rain quite heavily again, which meant once again changing into our wet gear.

The descent was slow and painful, and when we eventually got down to the car park at Square Corner, which is an obvious name when you see the place, we were well and truly soaked once again. A middle-aged man got out of a van to talk to us, and we thought he was going to offer us a lift into Osmotherley, but he just wanted a chat. As we stood talking to him, the rain got heavier, so we made our excuses and left, heading towards Oakdale Reservoir. We found ourselves descending some very steep steps which were now also quite slippery. A couple of times, I nearly lost my footing, saved only by my poles, and remember at one point I felt my knee joint bending the wrong way, which was discomforting, to say the least. Judging by the sounds that came from Rob, he had clearly had a similar experience. I was in front, but when I reached a small wood, I stood in the shelter of a tree and waited for him to catch me up. It was clear that we were both wiped out, and after a brief conversation, we both decided to look for somewhere to pitch the tent sooner rather than later. We had given up any hope of fish and chips and just wanted to find shelter, rest our legs, and go to sleep.

As we walked on, we weighed up the possibility of pitching our tent here and there. All we needed was a small 3-metre by 3-metre patch of ground, but paradoxically we could not find one. The area was very hilly, which ruled out most places. Bog ruled out yet more, and when we did find a small patch, a sign proclaimed private property. Passing some kind of dog kennel, we set all of the dogs barking which ruled out anywhere in that vicinity too. Finally, we found a field which seemed suitable, although it was full of cow pats, though gratefully, no cows. Did you know they poop 16 times a day?

I proclaimed it the worst campsite ever, but Rob was quite happy with it, so we proceeded to get the tent together. Perplexingly, the poles kept wanting to come apart, usually halfway through the tent as you put it up, which was annoying. It was next to some kind of barn, which although would not accommodate us, was okay for us to stash our packs in. The rain was now coming down pretty quickly all around us, and it was a miserable experience which foretold an uncomfortable, cold and wet night ahead.

This is not how I had imagined our first night of camping. The idea was that we would have a pleasant summer evening, and would spend time lazily but carefully putting the tent up. We would then sit outside because there would obviously not be any midges out in late August, where we would rub a couple of sticks together instantly creating fire using lint from my navel as kindling, and then eat our fish and chip dinner and chat the night away. The lint tip is an excellent idea, by the way, as it is highly combustible, but do make sure you remove it from your navel first. Incidentally, another good idea for kindling if you ever go camping is the guitar belonging to the hippy staying on the next pitch. Anyway, a nice coffee with a little something in it would follow, and it is this nightcap that would precipitate a refreshing and uninterrupted night's sleep for us both. Easy.

Once in the tent, however, the reality was that the rain sounded incredibly fierce as it seemed to pound against the canvas, and at the same time, the wind whipped up all around us. Torches came on, and we rifled in our food bag for something to eat, opting for beef jerky followed by chocolate for pudding. Rob had wisely brought along a flask of hot water which we promptly turned into Irish coffee and drank appreciatively. It was only around 8 pm, but it was darker than what it usually was at this time of night, presumably down to the bad weather. I took out my sleeping bag and unrolled it and started to climb in, as it was also starting to get a bit cool, although it was far from cold. Something was wrong, however. No matter how much I tried, I could not get in. It would appear that, by trying to save weight and opting for the lighter bag, I had brought my young sons *Power Rangers* sleeping bag, and no matter how many times I tried, I was never going to fully fit in it. Rob thought this incredibly funny, of course, but then he would.

I managed to send my wife a quick text message telling her that we had stopped for the day and were getting ready to go to sleep and how nice everything was, although I doubted that I would be asleep any time soon. I decided not to tell her about the sleeping bag debacle, the rain or the cowpats, as I was aware that she would be sat in our nice dry home, probably with the heating on, a glass of gin and tonic in her hands and laughing at me. By now, the tent seemed to be moving back and forth in the wind, and I sat waiting for the water to start dripping through with my shoulders and upper torso stuck clumsily out of the end of the sleeping bag.

At some point, I must have fallen asleep though, because I woke up to see beams of torchlight shining brightly against the tent. I wondered if someone was coming to complain about us moving in, and decided that I was not moving for anyone, but no sooner than they had appeared, the beams vanished. I did notice that the torchlight showed the outside of the tent was covered in spiders, though, which did not exactly thrill me, as I once read that there are 50,000 spiders for every acre in the countryside.

These torches reappeared a little later on, which puzzled me, as we were more or less in the middle of nowhere. I slept fitfully, waking several times more, including when Rob went to the loo and also to a noise that sounded like two hedgehogs having sex, which to be honest, is not the best sound to listen to when trying to get to sleep, though it beats Rob's snoring. I must have drifted back off again at some point, though, as when I next opened my eyes, it was light.

CHAPTER 3
Osmotherley to Clay Bank Top

I awoke around 6 am to the sounds of Robin rustling around. When he had woken up during the night, I distinctly remembered him saying *wow* as he looked out at the stars. I had a quick peek myself, and it was indeed a very beautiful and clear night. Sometime after that, heavy rain had set in once more, and I remembered lying awake once again waiting to get wet. The tent had remained dry, though, even through what sounded like a monsoon, though I guess that rain always sounds louder than it actually is when you are in a tent.

All in all, it had been a relatively comfortable night, and not anything near as bad as what I had expected. As well as staying dry, I had also been pretty warm, despite my sleeping bag cock-up, for want of a better word. Although my sleep had been broken and sporadic, I still felt quite refreshed. I had brought along one of those self-inflating camping mattresses, and this too had turned out to be surprisingly comfortable.

Rob had by now put the kettle on and was waiting for the water to boil, and I was just dragging myself out of my sleeping bag when the stove he was using started to emit giant flames that threatened to engulf the tent. He was wafting them down, somehow managing to not burn himself, and I was all set to abandon him and bail out of the back door of the tent when he managed to get it under control. He told me that he had mixed two types of fuel, and that was probably the reason for the inferno, and I wondered if one of them had been aviation fuel. His kettle had been left blackened and charred but, more importantly, we had hot water for our morning coffee, and the tent was not quite on fire.

Dragging ourselves reluctantly out of the tent, we surveyed our campsite by the light of day. It was actually a nice pleasant field, overlooking a shallow valley, though was still spoiled by the hundreds of cow pats that were dotted around. I imagined the bottom of the tent was not in a pleasant state, but on a positive note, the spiders had all gone. Slowly and carefully, we dismantled our little home from home and took it out of the field through a gate, where we hung it to dry in the early morning sun. Last night, the tent had been quite keen to fall apart as we were putting it up, particularly the poles, but this morning it had other ideas, once again the poles, which were reluctant to leave the tent at all, which is just typical. The rain had stopped though, which was a blessing, and meant that we could at least get the gear more or less dry. When we lifted the tent to check the bottom of the groundsheet, we discovered to our pleasant surprise that it wasn't too bad, and was only mildly covered in poop.

As we were packing up, a small group of joggers ran past. I say ran, but they were more or less walking, but in the style of running, if that makes sense, and clearly looked exhausted. It turns out they were running the full length of the Cleveland Way, in reverse, non-stop, which made me suspect that somewhere nearby, in a lunatic asylum perhaps, one of the warders was having difficulty finishing his morning headcount. Now I have mentioned before that I am very fond of walking, of the countryside and all that stuff, but to put myself through such a thing as a 109-mile non-stop run is not my idea of fun at all, so I just smiled and waved. Nutters.

All packed up and ready to go, we wobbled off down the lane towards Osmotherley, and almost immediately it began to rain. I was kind of looking for a better campsite nearby, just so that I could say to Rob I told you so, but there did not appear to be anywhere else that might have been suitable, so I just kept schtum. A couple of turns onto little lanes led us through what can only be described as a squeeze, where stone pillars had been placed incredibly close together and only allowed the thinnest of walkers through, and made no allowance for backpacks. The only way to get our packs through was to lift our backs so that they cleared the tops of the stone pillars, while simultaneously breathing in, which was challenging in the least. I personally took this as an attempt to discourage fatties from walking in the countryside, and made a vow there and then to shed some of my puppy fat. I reckon I must have lost a couple of stone yesterday, what with all that walking and not even making it to the chippy, so I must have been well on the way.

More twists and turns finally led us through a nice little snicket which suddenly brought us out into the centre of Osmotherley. It was still very early, so the place was very quiet, but we ventured to the cross on the middle of what looked like the village square and dropped our packs for a while. There was a sign for a public toilet which we intended to make full use of in order to freshen up, and there was somewhere to sit and drink our coffee, which by now would probably be cool enough to drink. I had read a bit about this place before the walk, and there are a couple of interesting things to say about it, despite it being so small.

Osmotherley is supposed to be named after some bloke called Osmund, or something similar. One winter, his mum vanished while out nicking firewood and when he went to look for her, there she was, as dead as a dodo, lying in the snow, as stiff as a board, so to speak. So, he lay down next to her and promptly expired himself as well, because this was where his mother lay. Get it? It's a bit of a stretch, to be honest, and I don't believe a word of it.

The village chippy, which I had been really looking forward to as has already been mentioned, is award-winning and was recently voted the best in the north of England. This is despite the owner, who had only recently taken it over, having no experience of running such a business. There was a lot of competition, but she battered them, apparently. Obviously, there were no signs of life at this time of the day, but I reckon I could even have eaten a nice big fish for breakfast had it been open, something which I would never have thought possible.

There is an interesting table next to the market cross, which is called the barter table, and is where we were sitting now. John Wesley, the founder of the Methodist movement, is supposed to have preached from here. I tried to find out some fun facts about him, but being a teetotal preacher and religious icon, this was always going to be challenging to say the least. The best one I could find was that he rode enough miles on a horse to circle the earth ten times. This was so he could spread the word of his gospel, of course, not because he was partial to a bit of horse riding. When someone asked him if he would consider walking instead of riding, he replied "Nay!". He is also said to have coined the term "agree to disagree", but there is a possibility that this is not true, as some attribute it to master potter Josiah Wedgwood, so we shall have to agree to disagree on that one.

Having both been to the toilet to freshen up, which was very clean and well-kept by the way, well done Osmotherley, we sat down for a few more minutes before moving on. A man with a drone was flying it up and down the high street, if you can call it that, and a couple of people had set up a stand of drinks which, presumably, were for the jogging extremists we had encountered earlier. A lady in a dressing gown wandered past, which sounds a bit random, but there was a camper van parked nearby where she eventually returned to. Putting our packs back on and moving off, I commented about the rather large covered and enclosed bus stop which could have made a suitable sleeping space last night, had we known it was there. I told you so, Rob.

Heading north out of the village, we followed the sign for the Youth Hostel, where we hoped to refill our water pouches. After walking for quite some time, we checked the map and found that we had not only missed the hostel, but we had missed the turnoff for the trail, which now lay around a mile behind us. There did not appear to be any way to rejoin it other than to backtrack, which we were not exactly enthused about, but we had no choice. Passing the Youth Hostel, we further discovered that it was down a long, steep road, so decided to get our water elsewhere. We finally found the turn off for the trail, with a sign clearly displaying that big white acorn, and wondered how on earth we had missed it.

Almost immediately, we came across a sign pointing to the Lady Chapel and went to investigate. It was not far away and was very picturesque. Apparently, it had fallen into disrepair and was largely rebuilt after the war, so the chapel you see now is not the original one, and this is evident if you take a close look at the stone blocks, with the larger ones at the bottom being the originals. Some of the 'new' stones were actually borrowed (stolen) from nearby Rosedale Abbey, which is a dodgy practice at best and another one that is probably frowned upon nowadays. It is a very unusual chapel in that it is semi-detached, with a nice little cottage next door, though there did not appear to be anybody in today. Finally, this little church had links to Catherine of Aragon, Henry VIII's first wife, so there you go. For anyone who needs a quick reminder of their history, Catherine had previously married Henry's younger brother, but he snuffed it after only six months, so she then moved on to Henry himself. Although she gave him a daughter, he wanted a son, so he divorced her, which then upset the Pope and, to cut a long story short, caused all sorts of trouble. Henry then tried to persuade her to go off and live the rest of her life quietly and out of sight, in a nunnery perhaps, but she basically told him to do one. Henry became convinced that his marriage to her was cursed, and that the bible said that any man who married his brother's wife would remain childless, despite the birth of their daughter Mary suggesting otherwise, and who, ironically having the last laugh, became queen herself in 1553. Now I know where Coronation Street get their plotlines from. You couldn't make this stuff up.

All historied out, it was time to once again move on, so we rejoined the main path and proceeded up the hill. The rain was on and off, but mostly on, so I just left my jacket on and decided to sweat. It was just too much hassle to stop, take off the rucksack, put on or take off the coat and put the rucksack back on again every time it stopped or started raining. I love this country, but sometimes I just wish the weather would make its bloody mind up. Foreigners often take the mickey out of us Brits because of our apparent obsession with talking about the weather, but I tell you one thing, if you lived in a country where you can simultaneously have a drought and a flood at the same time, and experience four seasons in one day, sometimes in one hour, then you too would probably go on about it quite a lot, trust me. It has often been said that the Innuit have hundreds of words to describe snow, which is actually not true because you simply don't need hundreds. But what is true, is that we do in fact have hundreds of words to describe rain, because we get so blooming much of the stuff and there are so many kinds. For instance, we can have a deluge, drizzle, a downpour or a drenching, and that's just for the letter 'D'. Oh, and I almost forgot about driving rain. The term raining cats and dogs originated here too because these animals often drowned in floods and floated down the street, making it look like it had actually rained animals. I could go on all day about this, to be honest, but it's time to move on.

Somewhere off to our left, behind the hedge that we were walking along, and down the hill that was behind it, lay Mount Grace Priory. I am not sure if you can usually see it from where we were, though I expect you probably could. Unfortunately, a foggy mist had shrouded the hill today, so at the moment we could see exactly nothing at all.

The Priory had at some point been bought by a wealthy industrialist going by the name of Lothian Bell. By all accounts, Bell was not exactly considerate to others, this coming directly from none other than the mouth of his daughter, Elsa. To back this up, there is an account of his coachman being found dead and apparently frozen *stiff on the box seat of his carriage*, and a further colourful illustration by the family biographer described him as *admired rather than loved*. He can't have been all bad, though. He had himself a mansion built, Washington New Hall, and when a seven-year-old chimney sweep died while working there, Bell abandoned the house and went to live elsewhere, leaving it empty for nineteen years, suggestive at least of some kind of conscience. And he did spend quite a lot of money doing up Mount Grace Priory.

Open fields ended, and we found ourselves skirting along the edge of a wood, which led past some kind of transmitter station, which had some of the most secure fencing I had ever seen. A dry-stone wall hugged our right, useful in that it served to block out at least some of the strong wind that had whipped up, seemingly from nowhere. At the end of the wood, the path turned to the right and began a descent down the hill and through moorland.

At the bottom, we crossed a road and began trudging uphill once again, through thick woodland. For a while, we saw a few more people, who all chose to park here for their short walks into the woods. A quick rest of our backpacks helped us along, as did some glucose tablets that my wife had stashed in my bag. This was Clain Wood, and we followed the contours of the land for a while before descending down a very rude incline, which gave my calves hell. At the end of this wood, we found a bench and were happily enjoying a break when more of the crazy joggers turned up. This bunch were very chatty and actually called us the nutters due to our impossibly oversize backpacks, and I think they may have had a point. A young lady also walked past with a pram, and we whispered good morning, as it seemed that she was trying to get her baby to sleep, and I found myself thinking that I am so glad that those days are gone. Robin then said that he could feel the mosquitos biting, so we packed up and moved on.

A left turn led us downhill through an empty pasture, at the bottom of which we forded a river because we couldn't be bothered to go up the three steps to the bridge. After a long uphill toil on a tarmac road, we passed a cottage before entering another wood, then turned right and up a hill onto what I would consider the classic landscape that you would imagine the North Yorkshire Moors to be. The next few miles were going to be a rollercoaster ride of ups and downs. We had both done this section before as much of it is also the route of the Coast to Coast walk, which although it is not a national trail as such, is one of the most popular walks in the country. The Lyke Wake Walk also shares parts of this route, and many people have told me that they have done this 40-mile walk across the moors non-stop and overnight. I wonder about the wisdom of this because you are not going to see anything in the dark. I am not just referring to the beautiful scenery, but I also mean things like cows, cliffs and big holes in the ground which sometimes try to kill us walkers.

As we got higher, the view became very impressive off to our left, looking out over the valley with Middlesborough to the far north. Whorl Hill stood out like a sore thumb with its forested summit, and if you squint your eyes or have some binoculars, you might just be able to make out Whorlton Castle somewhere to the left of it. A guy called Count Robert of Mortain lived here a long time ago, and while we may never have heard of him, it turns out he is the brother of William the Conquerer. There is nothing like a bit of nepotism and this is probably how Rob managed to become one of the richest landowners in the kingdom. It certainly wasn't through his business prowess, as he was variously described as both stupid and dull with a tendency to beat his wife. If you want to see him, he was immortalised on the Bayeaux Tapestry and is sat next to and on the left of his brother William, which means he is on the right as you look at it, but their names are on it just to avoid any confusion. He looks a bit shifty and seems to be nicking stuff off the table while the King is looking the other way, so he may well have been a proper Yorkshire lad.

More ups and downs led us to Carlton Moor, where we passed through two posts that seemed to mark the end of a very strenuous climb. The ups and downs continued, though were predominantly downs at this stage. The view was fantastic though, today especially, and we could see several storms raging far to the north and disappearing out of sight. None of them, hopefully, could be as bad as a storm that struck Carlton itself though, which is the village just down the hill to our north. In mid-August 2003, the day started out like most days that end in disaster, which was absolutely fine. But storm clouds began to build and by mid-morning, hail the size of gobstoppers was bombarding the village. The wind whipped up that much that it had the effect of sand-blasting the paint from buildings. Rain literally shredded the leaves and branches from trees, and a record rainfall of 49 mm fell in just 13 minutes. We know all of this because luckily the met-office has a weather monitoring station there. Yet you have probably never heard of this extreme meteorological event because it happened outside of the M25 and anyway, us Yorkshire folk don't like to make a fuss.

After what seemed like a tremendous effort, we eventually found ourselves down at the road at Carlton Bank and the almost famous café called Lordstones, and I am glad to say that the weather was great and in no way record-breaking. There was no question of whether we were going to stop or not, we didn't even discuss it. Rob went to get us both a drink, and once again I made the wrong choice. My plain, bog-standard coffee was well and truly outclassed by his hot chocolate, complete with whipped cream and marshmallows, and my subtle attempt to swap drinkies was soon exposed for the foolery that it was. The sun was trying to come out, and we certainly made the most of this stop. Rob asked the staff to put his phone on charge, then cheekily also asked them to fill our flask up with hot water. I am delighted to report that they were more than happy to do both without even a hint of hesitation, so a big thank you to the wonderful staff at Lordstones. We were also able to refill water pouches here, which was good as we were beginning to run low, although it did immediately add a few kilos to our backpacks. I wished we could stop here when I saw the lovely camping pods and luxurious bell-tents, but alas, this was not to be, as it was beyond our meagre budget.

After quite a substantial rest, we gathered ourselves together and got back on the path to head up to Cringle Moor. Passing a memorial to Richard, the creator of the Samaritan Way, we got to a gate where a nice young man held the gate open for me but then also waited for Rob to come through even though he was quite a few yards distant. Several people were commenting about Rob's oversize pack, this being a very busy stretch of path probably due to the easy accessibility of this area adjacent to the car park. At the top of Cringle Moor, we found a stone seat where we happily took a rest. A plaque pointed to everything you could see from this vantage point, including Ingleborough Hill to the west, Durham Cathedral to the north, and Roseberry Topping to the east, though cloud meant that the only thing we could see right now was the plaque itself, which was dedicated to Alec Falconer, a local rambler who was also a campaigner for exactly this kind of path across the moors, but who sadly died before it transpired.

Past Cringle Moor, and down some very steep steps, the path then went up again, this time to Cold Moor. This was definitely rollercoaster country, and after passing Cold Moor, we got our first glimpse of the Wainstones. I stopped for a moment to admire the view, and when I did stop, only then did I realize how quiet it was up here. There was no sound at all. No traffic, no voices and not even the wind could be heard. Someone, possibly that old bloke from *Karate Kid*, or perhaps the Dalai Lama himself, once told me that sometimes you find yourself in the middle of nowhere, and sometimes in the middle of nowhere, you find yourself. Anyway, it was someone wise, and it proved to be good advice. Actually, I think it was the old guy that sold Gremlins. Whoever it was, this was certainly that place. The middle of nowhere where you could well and truly find yourself.

Heading down once again, a sudden shower moved in very rapidly, and I soon found myself getting soaked. I stopped to do a quick change and glanced back at Rob, who was plodding along quite happily in just his t-shirt. I was in that much of a hurry that I had to put my two raincoats on in the wrong order. I usually like my thicker jacket underneath, and my cagoule on top. I find that this way, I am more likely to stay drier for longer. However, they came out of my bag in the wrong order and due to the severity of the downpour I just shoved them on. As I got walking again, and having a further glance at a coatless Rob just a hundred yards or so behind me, I came to the conclusion that he had just decided to get wet as it was not exactly freezing cold.

    The shower lasted all the way down the hill, which took a good fifteen minutes, after which the sun came out, and I started to steam. I stopped by a partially broken dry-stone wall and decided to hang my jackets up to dry while I waited for Rob to catch me up. To my surprise, when he arrived, he was completely dry, and looking curiously at the dripping idiot before him, said that he had not encountered any rain. This was at the same time as I stood there, right in front of him, not only dripping water onto the ground, but by now definitely steaming away in the strong sunshine, I was that wet.

    As we sat in the sun, a lady arrived and began to talk to us. She said her name was Karen and she lived in Middlesbrough. She was perhaps sixty years old, though it was hard to tell, and could have been many years either side of this. She was an avid walker she said, originally from Leeds but now enjoying life *up north,* which made me laugh, as I always considered Leeds to be well and truly up north. We discussed the recent lockdown, and she commented on how, at first, she had enjoyed it, but then had slowly but surely started to go stark raving mad, which is when she discovered walking. She said that since moving up here, she had initially not really gotten to know her way around, but had in the last few months walked more miles than she had probably ever walked in her whole life before this in an attempt to retain her sanity.

I understood what she meant, in a sense. Although I have always enjoyed getting out and about for a walk, so walking as such was not new for me during the lockdown, the number of walks certainly increased for me personally, and for most of my family too. This was evident in the local paths near my home. I have already mentioned that I had particularly always enjoyed the disused railway line which ran nearby, but at the height of the crisis, it had become unimaginably busy, forcing me further out into the wilds, which was difficult given that we could only go out for an hour or so.

She was excellent company, and we must have easily passed half an hour talking to her, but at some point, I suggested to Rob that we really should move on as we still had quite some ground to cover. She departed, and her final words were something about a gin and tonic she was going to have later and how she would make a toast to us in our filthy, damp clothes in our man-tent, just to rub it in I imagine.

We were now heading back uphill towards the Wainstones, an outcrop of rocks situated at the western end of Hasty Bank, and I have been told that this is the only section of the Cleveland Way where you have to use your hands. I certainly found this to be true. Although it is not a difficult climb by any means, it is certainly a scramble where you will want to take care. I had also been told that there is some Bronze Age rock art carved on some of the stones, but I could not see anything obvious today. I guess you would need to know where to look for that. At the top, I got talking to an old man who was up there bird-watching. He said he came up here every few days to keep an eye on a European Eagle-Owl, and he said it could at times be a bit nasty towards hikers, particularly those with dogs. He went on to tell me that it occasionally had a small deer for its breakfast, which raised my eyebrows a bit, but he also assured me that it did not generally dine on chubby old hikers, which was at least a small comfort, as their meat was considered chewy. I am not sure how serious he was on the last point, but I kept my head down after that. I have form with birds, you see, having once had my chin carved up by some kind of crow when I went into my garden one day. I remember it vividly, and I still have the scar today. This clearly corvid (as opposed to Covid) problem, is not necessarily the bird's fault, as they tend to attack anything that comes a bit too close to their nests, and a big blobby target like myself is probably quite hard to miss. I do not hold a grudge, however, as I quite like crows, but I couldn't eat a full one.

The view from the top turns out to be really good, what with the clouds having dispersed somewhat, and I stopped to take it all in while I waited for Rob. I could see down towards the village of Great Broughton to the north, which used to be the centre of jet mining in these parts a long time ago, so don't let anyone tell you that it can only be found in Whitby, because that is basically a load of old tosh. That is merely a bit of a marketing myth, but quite a successful one, on behalf of Whitby, regarded by many as the one and only source of high-quality jet, and the stuff became incredibly popular when Queen Victoria wore a lot of the deep black bling to mourn Prince Albert in the late 1800s. You probably also know that all of this lovely jet is a result of the fossilization of thousands of monkey puzzle trees over countless millennia? Well, I am sorry to tell you that you are plain and simply wrong and that this is absolute and utter poppycock. The confusion probably results from the fact that during Victorian times, all fossilized wood was referred to as *Araucarian* material. What with the scientific name of the monkey puzzle tree being *Araucaria araucana,* it is perhaps easy to see what happened, though I'm sure you already knew that little gem. Get it?

Roseberry Topping was now also very clearly visible, and we would hopefully be seeing it a bit closer tomorrow. We didn't hang about up here for long as we wanted to cover a few more miles, which was proving to be a slow process, to say the least. Descending towards Clay Bank

Top, which is actually and misleadingly at the bottom of a hill, we inched down what was for all intents and purposes one of the worst paths I have ever walked on. The confusion of Clay Bank Top is reinforced by nearby Chop Gate, which is actually pronounced Chop Yat, so from this we can only infer that the locals neither want you to know where they are or even be able to ask where they are. Anyway, some of the steps on this stretch were about a foot high, most were soaking wet and potentially slippery, and the gaps in between were full of fresh gloopy mud because of the recent rain that Rob had somehow missed. At the bottom, almost at the car park, the heavens opened once again, so we sought shelter under a row of trees with several other sad and soggy hikers.

It was gone 6 pm by now, and we had a conversation about whether or not it was worth it to try to get over Urra Moor before nightfall. We had to allow time to pitch the tent, and having previously walked over the moor and knowing the landscape up there, which was bleak, to say the least, we would have to get over the whole thing or none at all. There was no shelter on the moor, and the covering of heather across most of it made camping up there more or less impossible. We decided instead to try to find somewhere nearby to pitch the tent, so ventured down to the road for a look. A field on the right was quickly ruled out as it was marked *private property,* so we ventured left where we found a car park. A tempting patch of grass caught our attention, but it was right next to the road so would be very noisy and might land us a fine. I had heard that the local bobbies were patrolling the national parks dishing out fixed penalty notices to those hardened criminals that were wild campers. We dumped our packs down, and I suggested to Rob that we each go for a quick walk in opposite directions to see if we could scout out a suitable place.

I went up a small track that disappeared around a hill and after a few dozen yards found a spot that seemed suitable, so I came back down, told Rob, and back up we went. I timed myself on the way back, and it was less than a five-minute walk. There were just a few nettles on it that needed removing, and when this was done, we soon had the tent up. I figured we were developing a system.

This campsite was definitely better than last nights, being that it was off the beaten track and was not in a field full of shit, which is always a bonus. There were a few midges around, however, though I imagined there were not that many places on the moors that did not have them at this time of year. We got the cooker on and made ourselves some pasta, and Rob pulled out his flask that Lordstones had kindly filled up and we made another coffee, though this one had spiced rum as the magic ingredient as opposed to Jack Daniels.

All in all, it was a very satisfying meal, and

it certainly did the job. I had thought I would be much hungrier having walked all of these miles, but this was simply not the case. We passed the time away chatting about various things, and the sky soon began to darken, though once again I found it impossible to drift off to sleep while there was even just a hint of light. A couple came past walking their dog and said hello, but other than them, we saw no more people all night.

Sure enough, as darkness came, the rains began once again, and the wind was soon whipping around the tent in a provocative and intimidating manner. This continued for much of the night resulting in broken sleep for both of us. However, when you have walked many miles, often up and downhill, there is not a lot that will keep you awake for very long, especially after a nip of rum. I had some weird dreams that night as well, which were probably at least partially down to the anti-inflammatories I had before I went to sleep. Though I can't remember much about them now, I think they were good. Rob snored most of the night again, and after considering murdering him with the draw-string from my raincoat, I must have drifted off, and put this, too, down to the anti-inflammatories.

CHAPTER 4
Clay Bank Top to Slapewath

The day started with the heavy patter of rain pounding against the roof of our tent at around 6 am. This was good, in that it meant there was no rush to get up and about, so we could relax for a while longer. There was not much point in packing the tent and all of the other gear away in a heavy downpour. My legs were aching, and Rob had slept on a mound in the ground which had given him some kind of trouble with his back. A blister on one of my toes needed immediate attention, to which I applied a small compeed plaster, and another was threatening trouble at a later date, but not much later apparently. We brewed a coffee, minus any special ingredients, but did double up the dose so as to give us a caffeine boost.

After half an hour or so, the rain eased considerably, so we ventured out. We were surprised to see everything around us shrouded in a thick fog, but looking directly up we could see a hint of blue sky so hoped that it would soon burn off. I noticed a squirrel sat nearby on a rock and realized that I had been able to hear him chattering away for a while, although I had not really registered it. He did not seem very happy, and he jumped down and went to the corner of our tent and started digging our tent peg up. I rubbed my eyes in case I had maybe consumed some of those mushrooms that are not sold in supermarkets, but he was still there. We packed the tent as best as we could, shaking off as much water as was possible, all the while being watched by the little devil, but the tent was far from dry when put away. This did not bother us though as it would be back out in around 12 hours or so, and would not take long to fully dry, assuming the weather was half decent.

We loaded our packs and inched back down the steep hill to rejoin the main path of the Cleveland Way, with the squirrel still chattering away behind us, and I'm pretty sure he flipped me a middle finger when I wasn't looking. Once we got back down to the car park, where we had initially considered camping last night, we saw that it was now well and truly waterlogged. This would have made for a very uncomfortable night as well as a difficult morning, had all of our gear become wet. As it was, we were in fairly good spirits because we had managed to keep everything relatively dry, thanks in large part to Rob's bivvy bag, which had amply accommodated both of our backpacks and protected them from several thousand gallons of the wet stuff. To be honest, had Rob been a normal-sized human being, we could have used that bag as a tent.

After a short saunter along the road where a camper van sped past, whipping up spray and kindly giving us a brief but refreshing morning shower, we were once again on the path and, of course, heading up a steep hill. We were walking towards Urra Moor, and you may or may not be happy to know that there is a trig point here that marks the highest point on the moors, at 1,490 ft. This does not mean, however, that it is all downhill from thereon.

Once we were up the hill, which was not necessarily difficult but was a bit challenging for this time of the morning, the path levelled out. There are supposed to be lots of prehistoric remains up on the moor, but we only saw one. This was the face stone, which is what it says on the lid, a stone with a face carved on it. I took a look at it, and it was like looking into a mirror, with a squat, chubby face staring back at me. What I was more surprised to see up here was quite a large herd of cows, who were happily munching away on the best that the national park had to offer. It wasn't exactly a nice sheltered valley up here, so I figured that they must really like the grub available at this desolate spot, as there didn't seem to be any other reason to be here.

We were now once again walking through typical moorland, with the heather in its full August glory. Every now and then, a startled grouse gave us a bit of a surprise, choosing to fly away usually across our path as we passed, making an almighty racket as it did so. The odd rabbit scampered across the path too, and it was probably good hunting around here, judging by the several stone hunting butts we passed. I'm a townie and don't do hunting, but I have always wanted to try a bit of grouse or pheasant, but they don't usually have it in Tesco. The hunting season for red grouse starts on the glorious twelfth, so was well underway, but there were still many of the birds around. A curious law prohibits shooting them on a Sunday, and I found myself wondering if they could possibly know what day it was.

After around three miles, we got to Bloworth crossing and joined the old railway line that now serves as the route for this walk, where we began to head north. The sun was finally breaking through and combined with the now level and easy walking, it was turning into a nice morning. There was little to note at this point though, other than the odd sheep, as the landscape did not change at all, with heather moorland all around us as far as the eye could see. The path was straight, long, and quite frankly a bit boring, until that is, we came to Greenhow Bank.

At this point, the track started descending at an alarming rate, which is very unusual for a disused railway line. We mused that there must have been some cable system in operation at this point, as it was far too steep for any train to get up, and must have been a hair-raising experience going down as well.

I always think that walking uphill is hard, but it should also be appreciated that going downhill can be difficult too, though for different reasons. Exhaustion is my number one problem going up, but coming down involves challenges such as strain on the knees and ankles as well as trying to limit your speed so that you don't trip over yourself and skid along the gravel on your nose, which I have a personal and traumatic experience of doing when I was six years old.

All of these happened coming down this hill, bar the nose skidding, which must have only been about a mile long yet dropped around 700 ft in elevation. When we got to the bottom, we were tired and needed a break, and grabbed the nearest seat which in this case was a stack of industrial tubing. Each tube was maybe 1 ft in diameter, so it looked like it made a pretty good place to park. Rob dropped his rucksack first and went to sit down, climbing to the back of the pile for a more comfortable position. I was just advising him to maybe sit on one of the easily accessible pipes towards the front when the whole pile collapsed under his weight, and all of the tubes rolled forward a few feet. The rolling tubes advancing upon me threatened to take me out in a style reminiscent of the Road Runner getting one over on Wile E. Coyote, but I managed to thwart his most dastardly trick. Rob fell into what was left of the pile, but to be honest, he was that exhausted that he just stayed where he now lay, saying that it was actually pretty comfortable.

Greenhow Bank, also known as Ingleby Incline, was indeed too steep to be a traditional railway but relied upon an ingenious cable system where one train with wagons fully loaded would pull another empty train up the hill, according to the information board nearby.

People were not supposed to ride on these trains, but I have seen pictures of Victorian ladies all decked out in their Sunday finest sat on the back of a wagon and enjoying a free though somewhat risky ride up the hill. Close to her was a chap in a nice black suit and bowler hat, stood on top of the train as if it was the most normal thing in the world to be doing on a nice sunny Sunday morning. These people may have been the workers themselves, who lived in nearby cottages, some at the top of the hill and some at the bottom. The cottages at the bottom were clearly more popular, with the higher ones eventually earning the nickname *Siberia* for what are presumably obvious reasons. Accidents were frequent and often fatal, and presumably quite messy, and several people met a nasty end before the line was finally closed. The most common reason for an accident was a snapping cable followed by a derailment or two, which is presumably when the workers who lived at the top realized this location had its advantages and at least you would never get a fifty-ton train ploughing through your front window even though it might be a bit nippy up there.

We had a bit of chocolate to give us an energy boost, and I took out the map. I wanted to check the elevation, as I was pretty sure the route must be more or less flat from now on, at least for the time being, due to the amount of altitude that we had just lost. Something didn't add up though. According to the elevation profile that was printed on my map of the route, we should have dropped around 200ft, walked more or less level for a mile or so, then dropped a further few hundred feet. We had come down all in one go, though, which didn't make sense. We were still on the railway line, yet the picture simply didn't fit. Rob turned his phone on, which he had turned off to try to save the battery, and when it finally booted up, we checked the map. We were indeed still on the railway line, but we should in fact not be. The walk didn't follow the railway line.

When we had turned left at Bloworth Crossing, we did not realize that there were, in fact, two paths. We had taken the first when we should have taken the second, and unfortunately, they both ran parallel in more or less the same direction, giving us a false sense of security. I thought to myself that there was no way on this earth that I was going to trek back up that hill, a point on which Rob concurred, so we would have to find another way to rejoin the route somewhere down the line. Although this was a shame, we were not doing this walk as purists, well, not now anyway, and indeed it was the great Alfred Wainwright himself who said you should take your own route. I don't think he meant that you should get lost though.

Looking at the map, we figured we could either rejoin the path or alternately follow the road to Kildale, which was our first destination for today and also where we hoped to get some lunch, at the Glebe Cottage Café. We followed the track we were on for a couple of miles where we came to a small farm. A walker was getting out of his car and putting his boots on as we approached, and when we got to him, he asked us if we were doing the Cleveland Way. Replying that we should be but had taken a wrong turn, he gave us a couple of options to get back on the track. One sounded hard, and the other sounded, well, not so hard. Guess which option we chose? Not wanting to backtrack and climb up a steep bank, we went for option B, which was to follow a path through the woods, bringing us back on the trail a couple of miles further on. He also told us that the section we were missing was not the most interesting, so I presumed it was similar to what we had encountered along its parallel track.

We followed the directions he gave us, which immediately took us past a farm where some joker had made a very good scarecrow that had the likeness of death. There was one subtle difference in that it had the face of a sheep instead of a human, and a sign announced it as *the grim sheeper,* which I really liked.

All was great at first, though the path was a bit steeper than anticipated. We followed an old logging road, and I wondered how any vehicle could get up such a sharp, scrappy slope such as this. It was mainly loose pebbles, and where there were no pebbles, it was just wet mud. After only half a mile, the logging road abruptly ceased and turned into a footpath. It was not that well-worn, but at least someone had been along here, which was encouraging, as otherwise, it looked as if we were heading toward the middle of nowhere.

Rounding a bend, a deer strode across the path and disappeared into the woods with a graceful hop. As I passed the spot where it had vanished into the trees, I looked to see if I could see it, but there was absolutely no sign of it. The path was narrowing and getting a bit boggy underfoot, but we still seemed to be going in approximately the right direction, parallel with the ridgeline on which we presumed the proper path ran high above us. Nettles tickled us on both sides as the path evolved into a slow running stream, and I was glad to see my new shoes were doing their job so far in keeping my feet nicely dry.

A couple of times, I missed a step and saw my foot disappearing into something wet and smelly, but they still remained dry inside. We had slowed down considerably by now and can't have been going more than one mile an hour or so, but it was an exhausting hike and required a great effort to take each step. I suggested to Rob that this was possibly the hardest section of the walk so far, and he pointed out that this wasn't even the walk, or at least it shouldn't be.

Finally, I sighted a metal gate ahead which could only mean one thing – the end of this slog. I was elated to step back onto a proper dirt track, but this feeling did not last long. If we were to get back to the path, there was only one way to go, and that was up, which was becoming a bit of a theme on this walk. The track was impossibly steep, almost to the point where a ladder would be very much welcomed, and again I marvelled at what kind of vehicle could get up here. It was so steep that I imagined even a 4x4 would struggle, especially considering the loose stones that make up the track. Thankfully, this uphill slog did not look to go on for long, perhaps half a mile or so, but in retrospect, it certainly felt a lot longer.

I just put my head down and concentrated on making the next step, and when I looked up after a few minutes, I was dismayed to see yet more uphill hell. I vowed not to look up again as I did not want to see what was coming, but couldn't help myself. Rounding a bend, I did it again, but there was still no end in sight. Finally, sweating profusely and puffing like an asthmatic octogenarian, I rounded one last bend and at last saw the path flattening out where it met a minor road. Better still, a sign announced the return of the Cleveland Way and I even found a large rock where I promptly sat and dropped, literally dropped, my pack onto the floor.

Rob had fallen a long way back; he often does on the uphill. I walked over to see if I could see him, but there was no sign at all, so I shouted some words of encouragement in case he could hear me. I think I said something along the lines of *hurry up you tosser*. Finally, he hobbled into view and plonked himself down on the rock but didn't take his pack off and did not look amused. We decided to take a few more minutes so he could get his breath back and sat in more or less silence enjoying the view and trying to get our heart rates down a little. To be honest, I dared not say anything, just in case. I mean, he is a lot bigger than me.

A small car pulled up opposite us, and four pensioners got out, all masked up and looking like they were going on a robbery. I thought this a shame as there is nothing like the great outdoors and fresh air, so to wear a mask must spoil that experience somewhat. I said good morning and got a nod of a head back, and the pensioners wandered off to the south. A minute later, a huge logging truck appeared along with its support vehicle and stopped at the pensioners' car. The driver of the truck looked at me and pointed at the car, clearly unable to get past it as it was blocking the road, which was a sharp bend at this point. I shrugged my shoulders and pointed at the pensioners, who had in turn already seen what was going on, with one of them, presumably the driver, heading back.

The truck driver explained that another load was following him so he might want to move his car out of the way completely, which he did. The only problem was that the only other place to park was in a giant puddle, and as the old guy stepped out of the car, he looked very surprised when he heard a splosh and presumably felt a cold and wet sensation on his right foot. I tried to suppress a little giggle but failed miserably.

With all of the entertainment at an end, we decided to move on. The going was much easier now along what was a fairly recently laid tarmac road, though it was a little hard on the feet. We passed a small car park where the sole occupant was an old Volkswagen camper van and felt a little jealous about whoever owned it being able to live in such luxury. Apparently, you can somehow fit fifty people into those things as that is the world record, which would make social distancing a challenge, to say the least, and might even result in the odd pregnancy.

The road bent to and fro before dropping sharply to the valley below, where Kildale and the café awaited us. On the last stretch towards the village, the road flattened out but was hemmed in on both sides by high hedges. Halfway along this, a post office delivery van approached, and I secreted myself in the hedge so as not to get squashed. I thought the lady driving it gave me a nice smile as she passed and for a minute thought my luck was in until I realised she was laughing at me. I considered myself lucky that it wasn't one of the logging trucks that came by just as I was there, as there would not be room for it to pass without completely and utterly turning me into a mushy stain.

Arriving at the junction where the village started, I sat on the grass waiting for slow coach to catch up and had a little laugh when he emerged from the bushes immediately followed by a huge logging truck. He said it had had to follow him at walking speed for the last quarter of a mile and the driver did not look too happy, though at this point Rob clearly had stopped caring about holding up impatient drivers.

Kildale is a lovely little village, made more so by Glebe Cottage Café. We quickly found it, lying exactly on the route of the walk, and saw a sign with an arrow pointing to the garden area. We went around the back to grab a table, and things could not be better. The sun was out, we were halfway through today's walk, and we were about to get fed lots of lovely homemade scones and cakes.

I grabbed the handle to open the gate, but it was stuck. I tried it again but had no luck. Rob also tried, all to no avail. Slowly, ever so slowly, and somewhat reluctantly might I add, it dawned on us that the café was shut. 'No!' I screamed, with my voice echoing through the village and down the valley for several long seconds. I didn't, of course, but I wanted to. This was a huge problem. We were two very hungry blokes with a budget to blow, but more importantly, we were running out of water.

We climbed over the dry-stone wall and took over a picnic table to contemplate our little dilemma. Food was not so much an issue. We had snacks in our bags, which we quickly delved into, bringing out some beef jerky and some chocolate, which although they would feed us, did not compensate us for what could have been. Water was a more serious issue. Rob was down to less than half a litre, actually, scrub that, he just necked it off. Rob was down to nothing, and I only had a litre or so left. I promptly shared this out, and we both guzzled it there and then.

A hosepipe hung limply in a corner, so I went over to try it. Nothing. I knocked on the door of the café just in case it was one of these family businesses where they lived on the premises, but no one came. I could see a security camera on the wall, which I danced in front of for a few seconds hoping someone would recognize my distress and send out a rescue helicopter or arrange supplies to be air-dropped to us or something. Nothing. So, there was only one thing for it. I grabbed both of our water pouches from our rucksacks and decided to go door to door, begging for water. I was not sure of my chances. This was at a time when the general lockdown had ended, but there was still a lot of uncertainty, and I wasn't sure what reception I would get when I knocked on someone's door out of the blue. Add in the fact that I had not really had what you could call a proper wash for three days, and I came to the conclusion that my chances were low.

I headed up the road, out of the village, I think, where I could see a small cottage. I knocked and then moved a good few feet away to the other side of the single-track road. I saw movement inside, by the looks of it older people, and after half an hour or so, a lady with a kind-looking face opened the door. I apologised for disturbing her day and assured her I was not a homeless person looking for new digs or someone trying to convert her to one religion or another and followed on that her double glazing looked to be in excellent condition and was nowhere nearing the point where it would need to be replaced. I further explained our aquatic deficiency and wondered if possibly, at all, perchance, maybe, I could make use of that rather nice-looking hosepipe currently attached to the southern end of her most wonderful abode.

"Yes", she said and slammed the door.

Heading triumphantly back to Rob at the closed café, I felt like a successful hunter coming back from the forest and held up both pouches in celebration, wanting to scream *victory,* but managing to keep a firm lid on my immaturity. To be fair, we had everything we needed now, and should certainly be able to get a meal once we arrived at Slapewath and the much-venerated Fox and Hounds pub. As we were finishing our lunch, a family of four walked past and said hello and asked us how far we were going. When we told them that we were heading for Slapewath, they laughed and said we were pronouncing it wrong. We had been pronouncing it literally, but they said the correct way to say it sounded something like Slappeth. Good to know.

A couple of cyclists then turned up and tried the gate, and looked as disappointed as we were about the lack of food they were about to experience. Talking to them, they also said that they had food in their bags, and were going to go and sit in the churchyard to have their picnic. One of them was evidently a trainspotter, and he went into great detail about a stained-glass window at St Cuthbert's Church just around the corner. Apparently, someone had gone to great panes to make the window (get it?) which was by all accounts very colourful and featured a steam train, which admittedly is not your average subject for a stained-glass window in a little old English church. He explained that it was a reference to the Esk Valley line that ran through here. Interesting as it sounded, I was not walking anywhere to look at a window today. If I want to partake in that sort of craziness, then I can wait until I get back to Hull, where you will find England's smallest window at a pub I know well, The George, on The Land of Green Ginger in the city centre, which you have to admit is a curious name for a road.

Dinner done, we moved on up the hill with a council lorry passing us halfway up. We caught it up near Bankside Cottage and were surprised to see workers putting salt down on the roads, an odd thing to be doing in August. Amusingly, as they were putting it down, sheep were following them and munching the lot. I came across a dead rabbit, which sounds awful, but it had clearly been there quite some time judging by its desiccated state. It had also been flattened cartoon-style, and at some point, it had one of its ears cut-and-pasted near to its back legs, which gave it the appearance of a Picasso or perhaps even a Van Gogh artwork. I motioned to Rob that I found this mildly amusing, but he just looked at me in a manner that suggested I had perhaps sold his children or murdered his favourite pet and then eaten it.

The road only got steeper from this point as farmland gave way to woods, and at the top of the hill, a little acorn directed us left and up a hill towards Captain Cook's Monument. We found ourselves in a wood, which sheltered us from the sun that had recently decided to make a blistering appearance. The path meandered this way and that, and at some point, I felt sure that we were heading west, not, perhaps, the optimal direction to be going in on this walk, which ultimately led east and south. The path then decided that it had had enough of snaking through the trees and decided instead to head straight for the clouds. Muddy steps took us very high, very quickly, and the trees gave way to lush ferns before we emerged on to the barren hilltop that was Easby Moor, with the monument finally visible, though still a fair distance away. A boggy slog followed until we could finally throw our sticks onto the floor and drop our backpacks for a well-earned rest, which is exactly what we did.

The monument is impressive when you consider that some poor schmuck had to drag all of the rock up here to build it. The sun was beating down on us now as we sat in the shade to recover from the climb, and I couldn't possibly imagine having to drag rock up here and build something as well. We barely managed to have a wander around the monument and enjoy the view, which was excellent today though and well worth it. Great Ayton lay below us to the west, with Stokesley beyond that. Middlesbrough was to the north, spreading from east to west almost as far as you could see, and to the east and the south lay the moors that we had just tramped through. The most obvious feature, though, was Roseberry Topping, which stuck out like a sore thumb and looked absolutely splendid.

Great Ayton is, of course, the childhood home of Captain James Cook, intrepid adventurer and explorer famous for discovering Australia, even though tens of thousands of people already lived there by the time he arrived. Although he grew up in the village, he was actually born in nearby Marton, which is now a suburb of Middlesbrough, and many towns and villages around here lay claim to one link or another with Cook, including both Staithes and Whitby. By some lucky quirk, we will be going through both of these places, and as an added bonus, we will be doing this in the same order as Cook himself. His links with Great Ayton, though, are strong, and he lived there from a young age.

The Cook family home on Bridge Street was built by James' dad, being completed around 1755. It is well worth going to have a look at, apparently, so if you ever find yourself with an hour or two to spare and you happen to be in Melbourne, Australia, go and check it out because that's where it was packed off to in 1934. It was dismantled brick by brick and rebuilt twelve thousand miles away in celebration of Cook, so it is quite funny to find out that Cook never even lived in it, as it was only ever the family home after he had left home, so to speak. He may well have visited it, though, as can tourists now, who enjoy a tour around the antique-filled house accompanied by a period dressed guide speaking Yorkshire with an Aussie twang, which sounds kind of awesome and awful at the same time, mate. Incidentally, most of the antiques in the house have no link whatsoever to Cook or the house. And just to clumsily shoe-horn my home town in there once again, when it was finally taken apart for transport to Australia, the house was shipped through the port of Hull in a selection of barrels and crates, so there you go, and Hull is also where Robinson Crusoe set sail from, although not on the same ship of course. Back in Great Ayton where the house used to stand, you will now find a huge granite obelisk, which, satisfyingly, was built with stone that was shipped all the way from Australia, specifically Point Hicks, which is the first bit of kangaroo land that Cook ever saw according to some.

A young lady arrived with a feisty little dog which was barking at a much bigger, though also much more docile, labradoodle. I was surprised when she picked the dog up using its handle, which appeared to be built into its back, but which on closer inspection was a part of a harness that was barely visible. She wandered over and introduced herself as Jen, and we began to chat. She had a couple of pretty expensive looking cameras with her, and when I asked, she confirmed that it was indeed her job to go around taking pictures of things. I thought to myself that this was a pretty cushty little number, but you have to remember that this thought was coming from a guy that walked around all day and banged a few keys. It turned out that she was from the new generation of snappers though, and did not work for anyone as such, but was freelance and made money through the likes of Instagram. She said she travelled around and lived on the road and out of the back of her van with her little dog Jet. Jen and Jet. I liked it. Catchy, and somewhat appropriate. I told her that I had wanted to bring my dog with me, but he didn't want to ruff it. That was the end of that conversation.

The monument was quite busy, with lots of people coming and going, and amazingly someone turned up wearing a rugby top for one of two Hull teams that I am familiar with. This particular one was Hull FC, and Rob got talking to him first. I joined in, and he said he was up here for a week as they had been unable to travel to Benidorm due to the virus-related travel restrictions. I suggested that perhaps this area was better than Benidorm, and Phil, as he then introduced himself, agreed, adding that he would not normally holiday in England, but he was rather enjoying it and certain elements reminded him of Spain anyway, such as that the pool was cold and he couldn't understand the locals. After he politely declined our request for a lift back to Hull, and despite our suggestion that we had bitten off more than we could chew, he wandered off down the hill, as did we, although in a different direction.

We were heading north, towards the car park at the bottom of the hill and then on to Roseberry Topping. The path was fairly straight, and although it was steep in places, it was a hill, after all, it was not as bad as Greenhow Bank that had butchered our feet earlier that day. A couple of people commented on Rob's massive backpack and then looked at me disapprovingly. I knew what they were thinking, which was something like why are you making him carry everything, but we had split the load quite evenly. He had 60%, and I had 40%, which the last time I checked, were both even numbers, so in your face. Seriously though, I wondered what Rob had in his backpack that was so essential that he would carry it for 109 miles but had not seen signs of anything that really stood out, like a copy of the Guinness Book of Records for instance, or perhaps a nice shiny car-jack. I would have to take a closer look tonight to see exactly what was in there. The Holy Grail perhaps?

I was brought back into the now by a rustling and scraping sound behind me, followed by a few expletive type words that I cannot really put onto paper. Rob had missed his step and had it not been for his poles, he would be kissing the floor pretty passionately right now. I asked him if he was alright, but his face already and quite clearly told me the answer, which was no. He stood for a minute and then started to walk on it once again, but much more slowly and in a cautious manner. He seemed to walk it off, and after a further few minutes, we were at the car park where we grabbed a bench and took off our packs for a much-needed rest. Jen was packing or unpacking her van, it was hard to tell, and looking inside it was completely full of gear, even more so than Rob's backpack. Many families were also enjoying this area, and we sat in silence for quite some time enjoying the shade of the trees.

When Rob finally spoke, he said that he couldn't go on and that he was going to get a taxi to our finishing point for that day, which was, of course, the Fox and Hounds at Slapewath. He had done something to his ankle, and as we figured there was still another five or six miles to go, much of it hilly, he said he would not be able to walk that far that day. I considered going to ask Jen if she could drop Robin off at the pub as she had mentioned that she was heading north, up to somewhere near Lindisfarne I think, and might appreciate some cash in return for a favour. The elephant in the room though, of course, was coronavirus, as well of the usual problem of whether a young lady would feel comfortable giving a male stranger a lift, particularly a bald giant who looked like he had been living in the woods for three days. I decided not to mention this after all, and anyway, Rob had already found the number of a local taxi company and was busy dialling it.

He didn't have much luck with the first call. Whoever answered it did not perhaps have the best command of the English language and was clearly struggling with the Hull accent. Despite giving his location several times as the car park at Gribdale, they eventually put the phone down on him, the cheeky devils. The next two calls went first to a dead line and then to one of the more unusual answer-machine messages I have ever heard, which Rob put on loudspeaker, saying something like *I am home right now but just avoiding someone so leave me a message and if I don't call you back its probably you.* On his fourth attempt, Rob finally got to speak to someone who understood him, but the call still sounded challenging, and highly amusing, from my point of view. There was a problem in locating Gribdale, apparently, and they asked for a postcode which we obviously did not have. Rob asked them if they had an app called *what three words,* and judging by the half of the conversation that I heard, the answer was clearly no. They must have figured it out, though, because eventually Rob put the phone down and told me they would be there in half an hour or so.

I was going to continue the walk and meet him at the pub, and Rob offered to take my rucksack in the taxi with him. The thought of walking without that big heavy thing, the rucksack I mean not Rob, was indeed appealing, but I figured that I would need at least my water pouch as well as waterproof clothing, so just decided to carry my pack myself. I did unclip my mattress as well as my half of the tent though and gave it to Rob, which took at least a bit of the weight off, and promptly bid my follicly challenged friend a fond farewell. Rob did comment on the weight of the mattress and tent package, and I told him that most of it was probably down to the industrial-sized tent pegs he had put in, as well as, and I couldn't quite figure out why he had done this, the spare tent poles he had also popped in the bag.

I headed out of the car park and straight up a steep path heading towards Roseberry Topping. I immediately noticed the weight difference on my back and figured I would be able to move a bit faster as a result. It was now around 3 pm, and I hoped to make it to the pub before 6 pm so that we would have plenty of time to grab something to eat and then find somewhere to camp.

At the top of the hill, the path flattened out nicely, and I seemed to be making a good pace, that is until an older lady whizzed past me with quite some ease. I reckoned, though, that this was because she was carrying only a tiny pack which contained no more than a litre of water and was in no way due to the fact that I was an old and fat and very unfit gasbag.

Arriving at the point where the path turned off towards Roseberry Topping itself, I considered heading up to the summit but decided to give it a miss. Although it is technically a part of the route, it is only a spur and would mean a pointless return hike as well as quite a climb up and down. I have been up there before so figured that I was not necessarily missing anything crucial and furthermore, the only thing that I felt that I got from the first spur which took us to the Kilburn White Horse, was blisters.

It is an interesting hill though, and well worth a minute of your time. Many people have, over the years, described it as Yorkshire's Matterhorn, one of the highest summits in the Alps. I suppose if you squint your eyes and look at it on a moonless night with a bag over your head, then there may well be some similarity. Although it looks like it has a flat top now, up until 1912 it had much more of a conical shape, so to speak, which collapsed partly because of local mining. The hill is also possibly named after Odin, the god of war and death, which is pretty cool and good to know if it ever comes up as a quiz question. It is also said that James Cook was partial to wandering up the hill and it is this that is reputed to have given him his taste for adventure when he laid his eyes on the sea for the first time from the top of the topping.

The hill lies just within the national park boundary and if you are a fan of Chris Rea, who came from nearby Middlesbrough, his song Chisel Hill is dedicated to this place. Though not his greatest ever hit, he wrote this song at a point when he felt he had achieved his financial freedom, so it is a result of his artistic talents rather than an attempt to make loads of money. He still did pretty well from it, of course. He went on to achieve a UK number one hit in 1989 with Road to Hull, erm, I mean Hell and is one musician I am quite fond of if for no other reason than he is not your average rock star. He was even often mistaken for a stagehand in his early days, but took it in good humour apparently.

I turned right and was immediately met with a fine view across a shallow valley leading towards what looked like a forest. The path seemed pretty obvious, but I checked the map anyway as I did not want to get lost and have to do extra miles. The path led to a rough track for a while, before turning off back onto moorland and descending gently down the valley. It was easy going now, on what initially seemed to be ordinary paving slabs until I saw one that had been laid upside down. Thinking it to be an old gravestone, it was actually a memorial stone for a now-closed school. As I moved along, the downhill first became flat for a while, which was a relief, before once again becoming an uphill struggle. I followed a dry-stone wall and reaching a small wood, turned left. The path was still clearly marked, with those lovely little acorns directing my every move, although I had been told that once you got into the woods near Guisborough, it was a bit of a free for all with poor signage and many lost hikers. Not so today though, as I ventured into the main part of Highcliffe Wood up a gentle hill.

I am not sure what happened next. I can only assume that I stepped on a wasp's nest, as I was suddenly surrounded by what seemed like thousands of them. Now it is probably important to say that the best thing not to do in a situation that sees you surrounded by angry wasps, is to panic. I always tell my kids this and include the one great lie that they are more scared of you than you are of them. When you think about it, that statement doesn't even make sense. Anyway, I did the only thing I could do, and panicked. I flung my arms around my head to fend off the buzzing beasts, and I was sure that at least two of them had flown into my ears. I couldn't really run as such, due to being pretty knackered and still carrying my backpack. My actions only made them madder, though, and it was inevitable when one finally managed to sting me right in the middle of my forehead just as I thought I had escaped. If it's any consolation, I think that was the last thing it ever did, as I managed to hit both it and my own forehead with one of my walking sticks as I felt the sting, and almost knocked myself out. I came out of the trees probably looking like something that had been dragged through a hedge backwards, as the saying goes. Luckily, there was no one around to witness this little episode, and I trudged on.

Coming away from the wood, I found myself going up a small hill which provided a great view north and west, with Hutton Village immediately below me, and Guisborough beyond that. Although we were not going to venture into Guisborough, it is supposed to be a nice little place. In fact, positive accounts of it abound far back into history, with one of my favourites being written by a chap called William Derham, when he was writing about the life of a man called John Ray. He said, and I am going to have to quote him for full effect:

The people of Gisburgh are civil, cleanly, and well-bred, contrary to the temper of the inhabitants of Whitby, who, to us, seemed rude in behaviour, and sluttish.

I suspect he was not a fan of Whitby, but after reading this, I can't wait to get there. Anyway, the hill I was currently on and which overlooked the town was called Highcliff Nab, and judging by the number of people milling around up here, who all seemed to be staring at my forehead, it was a popular little spot. I didn't hang about too long but did enjoy the view for a short while, before carrying on with the vision of a nice cold pint forming in my mind.

The path soon turned into a forestry track and followed the edge of a high and incredibly steep ridge in what was now definitely Guisborough Forest. Two teenagers were sat on their bikes at the top of it, looking down and clearly pondering their chances of survival. One was encouraging the other to just go for it, while he presumably stayed safely at the top, the little sadist. Ignoring my temptation to wait and see what happened when one or both of them went over the top and plunged to their deaths, I carried on this way and that, trusting those little acorns that seemed to be at just the right places. The sunlight dappled through the trees and every now and then I would walk through a clearing before going back under the cover of some branches. I had hung my little solar panel onto the back of my rucksack and the combination of time of day and direction of travel, as well as the much-improved weather conditions, of course, meant that my phone was now getting quite a decent charge.

This wood seemed to go on for miles and miles, though pleasantly so, although it was in fact only around two miles from one end to the other. It was a very relaxing and calming stretch of path, as it usually is in the woods, and other than the boys on the bikes, I never saw another soul. I have always enjoyed walking in forests, and when comparing whether or not they are more relaxing than being by the sea, it is a hard decision to make. The sound made by the swishing of the wind around the treetops is similar, for me at least, to the sounds of the waves crashing on a beach and I could quite happily close my eyes and fall asleep to the sound of either. This kind of thing is becoming increasingly popular, almost trendy, and is even being prescribed by doctors as some form of nature therapy. The Japanese, who are well respected for being in touch with nature, even have a name for it – shinrin yoku. This basically translates as forest bathing, and if you relax, observe the trees around you and breathe in and out gently, I guarantee it will bring your blood pressure down. Indeed, it has been said that it is impossible to go for a walk in the woods and to be in a bad mood at the same time. Try it the next time you are grumpy, and you will see. I was doing this quite happily, enjoying the trees and the fresh air, when, far away in the distance, I heard the screams of two teenage boys followed by two loud crashing noises. I wish I had stayed and watched now.

The woods ended and I reflected that the path through it had been much better signposted than others had suggested. To my right were some farmers fields that had recently been emptied of whatever had been growing in them and ploughed back over. The path led down to another wood where I heard, but never saw, the sound of motorbikes. I was aware that there was an off-road motorcycle club around here somewhere and that the Cleveland Way passed along some of their tracks, which did not seem to be the best way of sharing a path if I have to be brutally honest.

Proceeding cautiously, I rounded bends and crested small hills, wondering if at any moment I was going to have a close encounter with what Bon Jovi calls a steel horse. I could still hear them, and am pleased to report that they not only remained distant but were becoming considerably less audible. I fumbled in my pocket to get my phone out, intending to text Robin, who would probably by now be sat in the pub enjoying a brewski, but missed my footing on the sloppy ground and tumbled earthwards, landing flat on my rear end and sliding precariously down a slope to what looked like a wet and sticky end in some kind of swamp. By some miracle, one of my trekking poles snagged a branch and arrested my fall, stopping me in my gravity fed tracks, but I think I still managed to land in dog shit and distinctly remember the taste of pine needles in my mouth.

It was of course at this point that the otherwise empty wood reached its rush hour, with ramblers simultaneously appearing from behind various trees and from both directions that the path went. More embarrassed than bruised, I hauled myself back up to the path after kindly declining any offers of help, my face a nice shade of red, where I stood still in order to send a text message. Rob had promised to get the drinks in once I let him know of my imminent approach to the pub, which was by my reckoning only a few minutes away.

I carried on and met a gravel road that presumably led down to Slapewath village itself, but after only a few yards was left confounded when a little acorn directed me back into the woods. I wondered for a moment if the trail passed by the village, but when I checked my map, it appeared to go directly through it, indeed more or less through the pub itself, which I thought a clever though cheeky marketing ploy to nab passing walkers. Back into the woods I went, and I could only surmise that I had misunderstood where I was and still had a little way to go. A little way turned into a long way, and it was a good twenty minutes before I emerged, battered, bruised and muddy, onto the main road which led from Guisborough to Whitby, with Slapewath just a few yards to my left.

There is an interesting spot just a couple

of miles to my right, though, which I must mention before we go on. It is very important, as it is reputed to be the burial place of none other than King Arthur himself. That place would be Freebrough Hill, an almost perfect sort of mound that you could imagine is man-made but is in fact entirely natural, and which looks a bit like the much more famous and definitely man-made Silbury Hill in Wiltshire. Lots of myths and legends have evolved around Freebrough Hill, presumably due to its arrestingly symmetrical appearance. Perhaps the best one though refers to a guy called Edward Trotter, a farmer from nearby Dimmingdale, who had a strange experience one day while out looking after his sheep. He is supposed to have found a hole in the side of the hill, and when he investigated it, it led him to a larger tunnel followed by a big oak door. When he went through the door, he was met by a man dressed in chainmail, behind which he could see a round table with lots of sleeping knights around it. The man told Trotter that these men were King Arthur and his knights, and they were sleeping here until England once again needed them to awaken. Sworn to secrecy, Trotter was allowed to leave, but he blabbed almost immediately to his wife, who brought him right back to check out his story. Finding nothing, she presumably reduced his beer ration for a good while.

Talking of beer, it was now only a short walk to the Fox and Hounds. Before I reached the pub, I passed a small picnic area that had a couple of tables and a small patch of land just big enough to pitch our tent, which I made a mental note of for later. Crossing the road, I spotted the pub and immediately saw Robin, who had not only managed to get a table but had managed to get possibly the best one in the beer garden, being right next to the door and directly facing the pleasant evening sunshine.

After asking him if that was the best he could do, I spied on the table a pint of coke as well as a pint of ale, at which point I dropped my bag, threw my sticks on the ground, and promptly collapsed into the empty chair. The coke went down immediately and enjoyably, but for anyone watching me, it was nothing like one of those diet-coke adverts where the hunky bloke necks it in one go. I spilt a bit as I drank it, so it was probably a sight more akin to watching Greenpeace pour buckets on some poor stranded whale somewhere.

Rob then told me that I looked like I had been dragged through a hedge backwards and asked me what I had done to my head. He then gave me the bad news; we would not be eating here tonight. I thought he was trying to have a joke, so went along with it for a while, expecting him to say gotcha anytime soon. It soon dawned on me that he had not done this though, and he was serious about not eating here. The place was fully booked up, and the only available slot was for the third Friday next month, by which time we would probably both have died of starvation. The government eat out to help out scheme basically meant half-price food, which explained this already well-renowned pub being booked up to the rafters.

As I sat there sipping my pint, one of the staff came out clearing glasses from the tables, and I struck up a friendly conversation with her. I explained our predicament, and that having walked a long way and what with the café at Glebe Cottage being closed and not having eaten for forty days and forty nights and how our legs were worn down to stumps, could they possibly feed us? She was very nice and said she would see what she could do but told us not to tell anyone. I felt momentarily elated until she came back with a piece of paper with some phone numbers of takeaways written on it, which knocked me right back down I can tell you.

A takeaway was considerably better than starving to death, we figured, so out came the phones. I had no signal, which was just typical, but Rob did have and promptly started dialling. Unfortunately, the quality of the call was not great, and he could neither make out what the other person was saying nor could they hear him by all accounts. For the second time today, someone hung up on him, which was quite frankly not only rude but was also a major impediment to us getting fed at some point.

Luckily, a young couple with two dogs were sat at the next table and had been listening to us and our predicament. They were called Lyndsey and Gareth and were very nice and presumably felt sorry for the two sad old wrecks that sat before them. He liked *Only Fools and Horses* and said that the only way he could get to sleep on a night was to put an episode on and shut his eyes. We talked about the episode that was set in Hull, I think it was called *To Hull and Back,* and I mentioned my own personal favourite which was the one where the chandelier fell to the floor. Immediately, he told me the name of the episode, *A Touch of Glass*, the year it was made, 1982 and then went on to tell us about other famous episodes, many of which I had long since forgotten but now came flooding back. I was impressed; the force was strong with this one.

Anyway, they had heard our dilemma, and in between trying to control their lovely and lively dogs, which looked like twins but were not, one was the uncle of the other, they offered the use of their phone. Rob dialled the next number on our list, but unfortunately, it just rang and rang without an answer. We thought the third and final number was going to do the same, but after around ten rings and just as Rob was going to hang up himself, someone picked up.

Again, whether it was someone who did not have English as their first language or if they were just struggling with the Hull accent, I forgot to ask so will probably never know, there were difficulties with the call. Eventually, though, Rob managed to impart to whoever answered the call that we didn't really care what pizza we ended up with, we just wanted some food. They then asked for the postcode of where we were, which we did not have and could not get, but after some lengthy discussion they finally, and dismally told us that they could not deliver to the Fox and Hounds at Slapewath after all as it was too far away, which was a bit of a bummer. By now, I think we had both more or less given up all hope of eating anything hot, and we resigned ourselves to going back across the road, setting up camp, and having some of our snacks for our tea as a meagre substitute.

We discussed this and more or less agreed upon it until Gareth said he would try one last number, which was his local takeaway. The phone rang, and we waited in anticipation as he spoke to the member of staff on the other end, told them what we wanted, asked how much it was, and everything else that you do on one of these calls, and it all sounded very promising. Unfortunately, at the end of the call, the takeaway insisted on delivering the pizza to Gareth's house, and no matter what he said, he could not seem to convince them to deliver it to the pub instead. In the end, he just said he would collect it, and put the phone down. They had said we could not pay by card over the phone and had to pay by cash, which was odd as most places were insisting on card payments during the pandemic. I have to say, when we watched them drive away with our £30, it did cross my mind whether we would ever see our pizza, but I dismissed this thought after a nano-second because they were such a nice couple.

Around half an hour later, they returned, not only with pizza but also fries and a large bottle of Pepsi, and we could not thank them enough. We offered to share, not only because we had ordered far too much, but also because they had been so helpful and had also been refused service at the pub on account of not having a booking. In retrospect, perhaps they did not want to share food because of the pandemic, but I suspect they just had food waiting for them at home, as they had happily shared their phone, although Rob had thoroughly wiped it before giving it back. This is probably a good thing because your average mobile has around 18 times more bacteria on it than your toilet. Just think about that for a minute. You have probably been told to wash your hands a zillion time a day, but has anyone told you to clean your phone? Go do it now, it's filthy. Anyway, as they left, and with a little chuckle, they told us we had been pronouncing the name of the place wrong. They said we should not pronounce it *Slappeth* but should say it exactly as it is spelt, so I now I have absolutely no idea which is correct.

When they had gone, we sat back in our chairs enjoying the last of the warm evening sunshine, and when the sun did finally dip behind the trees, we retreated indoors to escape the midges that were starting to emerge, so that we didn't end up donating blood one mosquito at a time. The staff told us that a storm was coming, and they were somewhat surprised when we said that we intended to camp out, but we interpreted their concern as that of people who are not used to camping out. We had another drink while we finished our pizzas, and then, grabbing our packs, we stumbled across the road to set up camp.

It was still just light enough to see, but we were shattered and wanted to go to sleep, so silently putting the tent up, we sorted our camp out, made our nightly cup of coffee with a little something in, crawled in our tent and went straight to sleep. The campsite was, in retrospect, pretty rubbish. We both got nettled quite badly, and the ground was both lumpy and waterlogged, but we were at the point where we had simply stopped caring. Rob snored all night as usual, but also made some noises from the other end which made the tent a bit windy. I had read that the top six foods that make you fart are beans, cabbage, cauliflower, corn, peppers, and milk. I reckoned that Rob must have had all of these on his pizza, followed by a nice big glass of the white stuff.

CHAPTER 5
Slapewath to Kettleness

We woke to the sound of a train crash, which was odd because there were no rail lines around here, and it turned out to be a different kind of wind to last night. Sticking our heads out of the tent, there was a storm raging outside which threatened to bring trees down around or even possibly on us. It is, in fact, a fact, that there are more tornadoes per square mile in the UK than anywhere else, I advised Rob, as we listened to creaky branches above our heads. It was still early, around 6 am, and we stretched and woke ourselves up while packing our sleeping bags and camping mattresses. It had been a broken, though surprisingly comfortable night's sleep, and what with the food of the previous evening, I felt that my body had recovered at least partially from its broken state of the day before.

Robin put the kettle on to boil, and we enjoyed golden syrup oats followed by a cup of coffee. We managed to pack the tent up and get our wet gear on in a gap between rain showers, which at least meant that our stuff kept sort of dry. We had considered having breakfast at the small café next to the Fox and Hounds, but it was still all in darkness at this ridiculous and early hour. Had the weather been better, we probably would have waited for it to open, but we thought it best to just move on and try to walk out of the storm. What we didn't realize, however, was that this weather was everywhere, and it had even been given a name which we would only learn much later on – Storm Francis. It was to bring down trees and power lines and would also break wind speed records in August for several parts of the UK. Had we known this, we probably would not have carried on, but as they say, ignorance is bliss.

Crossing the road and passing the Fox and Hounds for the last time, the path went straight up a very severe slope which can only be described as an unwelcome start to the day at best. Annoyingly, after the first flight of steps, we came to an open area that looked like it had once been a quarry, and would have offered a far superior, flatter and drier campsite the previous night. This made me pretty grumpy, and I thought I had better keep quiet, but I heard Rob say *I told you so* and caught him giving me that look again, the one that said *you killed and ate my pet*.

We carried on up the hill further, and the

going became easier and less steep, leading us through a wood which sheltered us from the wind. The rain had more or less stopped, though we still felt the occasional drop, but this did not last long. As we emerged from the trees, we found ourselves on a wide-open plateau where the wind buffeted us from our left, which meant it was coming from the north. As my hat almost blew off, I reacted at a speed that surprised myself, saving me from a muddy run after it through a field of crops. Shoving it into my jacket, the rain came back with a vengeance, and it felt similar to what I imagine it would feel like to be sand-blasted.

This persisted for a mile or two until we reached the shelter of some houses and a hedge, which signified the beginning of Skelton. There was nobody around, probably because of the wild and wacky weather, though I imagine it was hardly a bustling metropolis at the best of times. We went past a small skate park where I suggested to Rob that we should do a quick circuit so as to keep our fitness levels up, what with us not having had any exercise lately. We then found ourselves on Swilly Lane, where some local prankster and outright genius has painted white gloss over the 'S', which gave us both a much-needed chuckle on this very gloomy day.

This was perhaps the same prankster who had a poo in the visitors' book in the local church, Old All Saints, a while back. I kid you not, someone actually did this. One cold and damp January in 2019, the custodian of the church, John Connelly, returned to the building after running a fundraising event at the church hall and found bits of poo scattered about as well as in the guest book. The poopy perp had also set fire to a postcard rack, which had thankfully burned itself out, and, get this, buried the postcards for sale notice, which I find just a tad random and suggestive of a screw loose if I am brutally honest. If you're passing, the church has one other claim to fame, and this one is probably worth looking at. If you wander around the graveyard, you will find some gravestones bearing skull and crossbones motifs, which is quite frankly a bit spooky and very mysterious. I wish I had time to go and have a look, but it is a bit out of the way today, so we shall plod on.

Suddenly, and without warning, the high street appeared ahead and below us, which was unfamiliar territory on this walk, having spent nearly all of it in a much more rural environment. To my left, I could see what looked like a small garden and shouted to Rob that I wanted to have a quick look. I had seen a small statue and wanted to see what it was, or who it was more specifically. When I got to it, I was surprised to discover that I recognized the name, if not the face. It was Frank Wild, a fairly well-known Antarctic explorer, who apparently came from around here. I say fairly well-known Antarctic explorer, but this is a subject that I love, and I am a bit of a geek when it comes to such matters.

Anyway, after doing some digging, it turns out that Frank Wild has an interesting story to tell. He was indeed born in Skelton, in 1873, and after a brief career in the merchant navy, decided to get into the exploring business. His mum Mary, with her maiden name of Cook, had always claimed her ancestry back to none other than Captain James Cook himself, although this is unlikely as Cook has no known descendants, so I'm not sure where she was going with that one.

In 1901, Wild went on Captain Scott's famous expedition that kicked off the so-called heroic age of Antarctic exploration. This is where he first met the much better-known Ernest Shackleton, whom he would later accompany back to the frozen continent. He also went on Douglas Mawson's famed Nimrod expedition in between, which further helped to build his reputation. This was despite Wild's first impression to Mawson being that of a drunk getting thrown out of a New Zealand hotel, which is not an ideal first impression to make in any new job, it must be said.

Later on, Shackleton had reportedly placed an advert in the press requesting men for his 1914 expedition and said that it would probably be a suicide mission. Okay, what he actually said was *Men wanted for hazardous journey. Small wages, bitter cold, long months of complete darkness, constant danger, safe return doubtful. Honour and recognition in case of success.* This is about the same as you can get to calling it a suicide mission when you think about it. Anyway, although it was not exactly the most positive job description ever, it did the trick, and Wild signed up.

Wild had worked his way up the chain and had by now become a senior, well-respected explorer himself, and in August 1914, they finally set off. However, within a few days, the ship encountered heavy pack-ice, and after just a few weeks, it had become trapped completely. The ship and its crew spent most of 1915 stranded, and despite some signs of the ice breaking up, disaster finally came, and the ship was crushed by the ice in November. The crew salvaged what they could, made camp, and came up with a plan to escape. Shackleton would take some of the men with him on an 800-mile sea voyage to South Georgia, where they would find a whaling station and with it, the possibility of rescue. Easy.

So it was, in April 1916, Shackleton left Wild in command of their small camp on Elephant Island and set off north in the lifeboat that they had salvaged. Wild looked after his men well, keeping every single one of them alive for almost four months, surviving on a meagre diet of seals and penguins, until Shackleton finally returned with a rescue boat. They did not reach safety until September 1916 though, over two years after setting off. I often wonder what Wild thought when after returning home, he would inevitably at some point have seen some of the common or grey seals that are so common along the Yorkshire coast. Yummy perhaps? Probably not.

You would think that his experiences would have put him off, but Wild once again joined Shackleton a few years later, on the 1921-22 Shackleton-Rowett Expedition, and was by now essentially Shackleton's right-hand man. Once again, things weren't exactly tickety-boo, and to cut a very long but interesting story short, Shackleton died of a heart attack on South Georgia, which can certainly be described as a sub-optimal outcome. His body was shipped all the way to South America, where they received a message telling them to bury him on South Georgia, so they sailed all the way back again. He was eventually buried on the remote island at Grytviken Cemetery, and Wild sailed on, completing the mission.

After this, Wild presumably decided he wanted a more agreeable climate, and settled in balmy South Africa, where he could still presumably enjoy his diet of seals and penguins had he wanted to. He had mixed fortunes and suffered along with everyone else during the Great Depression. He died in 1939, and it was his wish to be buried alongside *the boss*, as Shackleton was by then affectionately known, on South Georgia. However, the Second World War had other ideas in store for him, making such a burial impossible.

Basically, he was cremated, and his ashes vanished after his widow passed away a little bit later. As is the tradition of saving the best till last, here, indeed, is the best and last of this story. In 2011, his ashes were found in the very place that they had been all along, and in fact in the place that they were supposed to be, had anyone bothered to look, at the Braamfontein Cemetery where he had been cremated. They were found by British historian and author Angie Butler, and on 27 November 2011, Wild was finally laid to rest next to *The Boss* at Grytviken Cemetery in South Georgia, 72 years after his death, and on his right-hand side.

After spending a few moments telling Rob this story, it was time to move on, so I woke him up. The urban environment had, however, already stumped us, and I wondered how the lack of signposts, which had been so plentiful along our route so far, would affect our navigational skills. I was about to check the map but then noticed a little acorn on the opposite side of the road, which was different from every other signpost up to this point. The rest had all been wooden, mounted on a post, with an arrow pointing in the desired location. This one, however, was a small metal looking sign mounted high on the wall of the shop opposite and would be easy to miss, which we almost did.

Carefully crossing the busy road, we were directed onto a housing estate where all of the street names seemed to have a Lake District theme. We found ourselves variously walking past Derwent Road onto Coniston Road, and then down Ullswater Drive before realizing we had taken a wrong turn. As I was checking the map, Rob's phone rang, and it turned out to be his priest of all people, and as the conversation went on and Rob told him where he currently was, it transpired that he was from around these parts and knew the area well, which was a spooky though handy coincidence. Directions in hand, we moved on, contemplating this funny old world where sometimes things happen for a reason.

We rejoined the Cleveland Way which left Skelton heading north past a street bizarrely called *No Ball Games* before a small tunnel led us under a road and into Crow Wood, where there was a definite lack of crows, it has to be said. A group of ladies was heading towards us, and as they were going uphill, we decided to give them priority and moved out of the way. Some of them were wearing face masks, which I had not considered necessary outdoors, but each to their own, I thought. I realize some people in vulnerable groups need to take every possible precaution, and I am always the last person to judge others.

While we were waiting, I discussed with Rob whether or not countryside etiquette meant giving priority to people heading uphill or downhill. I think that I came down on the side of giving priority to those heading up, as they are probably tired and finding it hard going, though I can see the argument for giving it to those heading downhill in that they can't stop and might well be a human missile. While we are on the subject, I often find it funny that some people simply refuse to give way, and barrel through you as if you are not there. I have, on occasion, found myself looking up to see someone worryingly close, despite having definitely seen me, but choosing to neither move to the other side nor stop. Usually, the best and often the only course of action is to dive into a thicket of nettles, or perhaps a holly bush, which in this day and age has to be safer than breaching social distancing guidelines, we are told.

These ladies were all very friendly and polite and stopped to talk to us. One of the ladies who had a mask on was talking, and I found it difficult to understand her, though managed, just. They were all observing a reasonable social distance, as were we, which goes to show that you can, and indeed should get out there and talk to strangers, despite the current so-called *stranger danger*. My own way of thinking on this, and I may well be wrong so please don't quote me, is that the danger of a pandemic and any actions deemed necessary must be balanced with the need for a meaningful and satisfying life. Many people found it difficult to cope during the darkest days of the lockdown, a story which will at some point, but not yet, be told through that very dark but now so familiar phrase of *excess deaths*, particularly those deaths that cannot be attributed to the virus itself.

Once the ladies had all passed, we carried on down the hill and at the bottom we came to a small bridge crossing Skelton Beck. It was in full flow today and had I not seen the name on the map, I would have presumed it to be a proper river. Looking up, and towering over our heads, and yes, even Rob's, was the impressive sight of Skelton Viaduct.

After this, the path turned upwards again, taking us slowly but surely along the valley of the beck towards Saltburn, or to give it its proper name, Saltburn-by-the-Sea. Every now and then we heard the whistle of what sounded like a steam train, though I wondered if it was something to do with one of the museums around here. We emerged from the woods more or less in the middle of the town, just a quarter of a mile from the train station, where we immediately headed to get out of the rain that was once again falling all around us. As we got nearer to the station, the wind began to pick up, which made the rain hitting our faces once again quite painful.

When we arrived, I dropped my bag somewhere dry so I could get an extra waterproof out of it, and while I was at it, I grabbed a snack as well. Rob waited to be seated at the café, while a busker played sea-shanty type songs and it was all very pleasant. When I went over to join Rob, a young lady came out and told us we needed a reservation, but then immediately back-tracked as a couple left their table just at the right time. We ordered a sandwich and a drink, Rob once again going for the hot chocolate while I grabbed a cappuccino, which I hoped would give me an afternoon caffeine boost. The sandwiches were okay, clearly freshly made, but they did not fill the gap that their price would suggest.

Saltburn is a tidy little place, even on a windy day like today. It has a pier, the only one in Yorkshire apparently, but when it was built it was not very popular. This is probably because you had to abseil down quite a high cliff to get to it, so in 1884 a cliff-lift, or tramway, was built to take lazy tourists to and from the beach and of course the pier. When I had read that Saltburn Pier is also the most northerly pier in Britain, I assumed that some cretin had made a mistake and meant England. It is with some surprise, then, that I spent a considerable amount of time trying to find out if there were any piers in, say, Scotland. Apparently, there are none, well, not proper ones anyway. I had to sit down and have some smelling salts at this news. No piers in Scotland, and in fact none north of Saltburn. Could this really be so?

Apparently, yes. There are one or two contenders, but they are either wrecks and abandoned or not recognized as piers by the pier police. I think this seriously sets back any hope for independence that our friends the North Britons have if they cannot even muster up a single solitary pier between them. These non-pier builders are also the ones who spent £125,000 on devising a new slogan to attract tourists in 2007. The winner was *Welcome to Scotland*, but it's okay, because it was only taxpayers money. The Scots did, however, manage to fend off the Romans, which few people at the time managed to do, it has to be said, which completely redeems them, in my eyes at least. Anyway, a quick check with the National Pier Society, yes it really exists, says that there are only 61 piers left in the UK, and this one is indeed the only one to be found in Yorkshire.

Outside, the rain lashed the pavement, and we could hear the wind howling around the windows and the doors. I think we both could have quite happily sat there for the afternoon, in the warmth and with some pleasant music drifting into our ears, but once we had finished, we thanked the staff and asked for the bill. It was at this point that they told us it was cash only, which was a problem, though luckily there was a cash machine outside. As we left, I found myself thinking that it was odd that two places on the trot had required cash payment, at a time when most businesses were insisting on card payments for hygiene reasons. I mentioned to Rob the possibility of a problem with the network, though this seemed unlikely as the cash machine was working fine. Anyway, as soon as we stood up to leave, another group immediately grabbed our table. This place was clearly doing a roaring trade.

As we left the café, I got a sense of what

it must be like to jump into a washing machine mid-cycle. For one minute, I wondered if someone had placed a bucket full of water above the door just for a laugh. We immediately got sprayed with stinging rain, and the wind tugged us to and fro and almost brought us both down until we managed to find our balance. We found our way through the streets, past some fine old Victorian houses which were probably holiday lets by now, towards the seafront, where the wind picked up even more. Shortly after this, we got our first up-close glimpse of the North Sea, which was today looking a tad stormy, to put it mildly.

My mother-in-law had recently asked me why the name of this sea had changed from the German Ocean to its current name, and the answer is simply politics, though perhaps simply is not quite the right word to use. Incidentally, I had first come across the old name, the German Ocean, when I read *The Invisible Man* by H.G. Wells many moons ago, but I have to admit that I did not get the link at the time and thought it might even have been a made-up name.

Up until around the mid-1800s, both names had been used interchangeably, but the North Sea slowly though gradually gained prominence, particularly after 1850. In 1898, Germany enacted something called the Fleet Act, one that basically aimed to bring the Imperial German Navy up to parity with the Royal Navy.

This was a clear challenge to the dominance of the British Empire and greatly upset the top-brass at the admiralty who were having none of it. For the British, who now figured that the name of a body of water also signified strategic dominance of it, the old name now became intolerable. Subsequently, the British press became particularly reluctant to use the old name for fear of being unpatriotic, and the First World War made its use potentially treasonous and sealed its fate forevermore for it to be known as the North Sea. This meant that by the 1920s, the old name was dead in the water, so to speak.

Interestingly, the Germans had never called it the German Ocean but had always used Nordsee, or North Sea anyway, so it was perhaps just a domestic thing for the Brits. It is probably important to say that the British Royal family also changed their name at around the same time, from the distinctly suspiciously foreign in general, and German in particular sounding Saxon-Coburg-Gotha, to the much more amenable and English sounding Windsor, in 1917, so there you go.

Carrying on through the town towards the sea-front, we saw a couple of pubs dotted here and there, but if you had popped by for a drink any time before 1982, then you would have been well and truly stuffed. This place had originally been founded by Quakers, and it remained pub-less right up until just before Christmas of that year, which presumably resulted in one heck of a party and the odd hangover or three.

Despite being pub-less in the olden days, though, there was, in fact, the odd party known to be happening in the 1800s in Saltburn, and one presumes that the participants must have smuggled their own booze in. Some visitors were quite high profile and included none other than a future King. Edward VII, though still a prince at the time and married to Princess Alexandra of Denmark, used to come to the town to spend some quality and quite athletic time with a well-known actress, Lillie Langtry. This was partly because his mother, Queen Victoria, had been on the throne for what seemed like forever, and he, therefore, had nothing else to do, which has a modern twist to it, if you think about it. They stayed at a place called The Nook for, well, a bit of nookie.

Finally, before we leave Saltburn, I have to mention that it is the birthplace of none other than David Coverdale, lead singer of Whitesnake, a very well-known band from my youth and one of my favourites. He had a very impressive head of hair, and I often think that I wish I had hair like that, while Rob just wishes he had some hair. But enough of that, it is time to walk on, and with Rob far behind me, here I go again on my own.

We turned right and began to follow the coast, which meant that we were now on the second stage of the walk, which is generally split by most people into the inland section and the coastal section. This also meant that we were now heading home, quite literally, with every step being a step nearer to our final destination of Filey, and after that, a bath and clean socks. Many people had told me that they had enjoyed the coastal section more than the part over the moors, so I was particularly looking forward to the next few days. It had been hard going so far, and I was also told that the level of effort required eased off a little along the coast, which would be more than welcome.

To our left, the North Sea whipped and whirled, with ginormous waves constantly crashing against the sea-wall. There was no sign of the pier, which puzzled me, and I momentarily wondered if it had been washed away that very morning. Looking at the rough seas, this would not have been surprising in the slightest. A little further on though, it finally came into view, and I was surprised to see that people were on it, despite the waves carving over the top of it, and wondered whether or not Yorkshire really would soon be pier-less due to the crazy weather. We also found the tram lift, though it did not appear to be operating today, for obvious reasons.

Looking down on the beach in such stormy conditions, it is hard to imagine that Malcolm Campbell, journalist, soldier and general lunatic, once attempted to break the world land speed record at this very spot. In 1922, he drove his car Bluebird along the sands at an amazing 138 mph, but unfortunately, this was an unofficial attempt and did not count, which seems one heck of a risk for absolutely nothing. He nearly died here that very same year, when he was bombing along at 134mph, and a dog ran out in front of him, such was the lack of organization at the time that saw tens of thousands of people stood on the sand during each attempt. Although Malcolm was quite famous, his son Donald was perhaps much better known. Unfortunately, however, he is best known for dying during a water speed record attempt on Coniston Water in the Lake District in 1967, also in a craft called Bluebird. I was later surprised to find out that Malcolm had been a bit of a closet fascist, though, despite him having being knighted by King George V. Who knew?

Anyway, the beach below was used for land speed records for much of the first half of the 20th century and beyond, by many other than just Campbell alone. Many prominent nutters attempted suicide by driving recklessly along the sands at speeds that I wouldn't even try nowadays, in what would inevitably be a much safer car. Algernon Lee Guinness, the brewery heir, was one such curiously named fool, who came here many times, including a trip in what was at the time the world's fastest car. This French-built Darracq, a 200 horse-power monster, looked a bit like it had a missile strapped to the top of its engine and went like one too, and would have been at home being driven by Dastardly and Muttley. It looks a bit like Chitty Chitty Bang Bang stripped of all its body panels, and if you haven't seen that film, go watch it now, it's ace, and then watch Dastardly and Muttley. Strangely, 200 horse-power does not mean a car has the power of 200 horses, which I always thought to be the case. Confusingly, a horse has a horse-power of about 15, which is just plain silly when you think about it.

A steep hill took us down to the bottom of a dip where we met a road that seemed to come down and straight back up again for no obvious reason other than geology, or is it geography? No, I think it's geology. Anyway, I passed a small, old building behind the Ship Inn that looked disused, and realized belatedly that it was the old mortuary, and considered whether or not we should just drop ourselves off there now, and save all the hassle. Next door to the Ship Inn, there used to be a museum about smuggling, but testament to the power of the sea, it was severely damaged in a storm and is probably gone forever. It turns out that the pub itself had been the original mortuary, but the multitude of bodies that kept washing up on the beach eventually resulted in what stood before me now. I imagined going into the pub in the olden days, ordering my pint and then clambering over a couple of bodies to claim the nice spot next to the fire. Hmm, actually, come to think of it, I think it's definitely geography.

The Ship Inn had also been the centre of smuggling in the local area, with the most notable participant being a Scotsman by the name of John Andrew. In the late 1700s, Andrew took advantage of the cliffs and coves that abound up and down this coast, and subsequently became known as the King of Smugglers. High taxes on tea, gin and brandy, among many other things, had been imposed in order to pay for various wars against France and America and anyone else who was up for a scrap, but the locals clearly had other ideas. Whole villages often turned out to help unload illicit cargoes in the middle of the night, before the excisemen had chance to get to what were relatively remote locations way back then.

Once goods were ashore, they could quickly disappear into the narrow streets, and many houses even had secret rooms within which smugglers could hide both themselves and their contraband. Tales also abound of old ladies hiding kegs of gin in their bloomers or mothers cradling jars of spirits in babies swaddling and walking right past the customs men, which is just fab.

Andrew was a particularly canny man, though, and with quite a high social status, he managed to secure himself a position in the local militia, which was often involved in searching for the smugglers. This effectively meant that he was looking for himself, which also meant that he was very unlikely to get caught, though he did eventually spend some time locked up after being caught on a run at Hornsea. This picture of loveable rogues and local heroes is far from the truth in reality, however. Violence was common, and the tales that have been passed down have simply omitted some of the harsher acts that went on.

Back in reality, the path struck skywards again at an alarming rate. As we got higher, the wind picked up even more, and it was becoming difficult to stay upright. I seriously considered the practicality of continuing to walk in this weather, which was very much borderline, and it was only the direction of the wind that swayed me, both figuratively and literally. It was blowing towards the south-west, which meant that for all intents and purposes if the wind did catch us, it would merely blow us into a field rather than off of a 200 ft cliff towards a splashy though swift death, which would offer only a couple of seconds for that famous flash-back of your life you are supposed to get when you croak.

At the top, the path more or less levelled out, as did the wind, although unfortunately it levelled out at around 50 miles per hour. You would think that a back wind would help you move along at a bit of a quicker speed, but I reckon that any benefits from back winds disappear at around 20 or 30 miles per hour. Above that and you just find yourself in a fight to stay upright, and once again, it was our sticks that were helping us to do so. Every now and then a gust would come along that would be so strong, you would find yourself literally stopped in your tracks and unable to move, with your sole purpose being to remain standing at that point in time and to try to stay alive. Occasionally, when moving your trekking poles forward, the wind would even take them, which would again stop you in your tracks, as it was impossible to retain your balance without them. I was very surprised at the ability of the wind to blow our sticks around as they were, as it says on the box, just skinny sticks. I guess it was because they were so light.

Walking in these conditions was quickly becoming exhausting, and after a few hundred yards I took advantage of a wooden fence to rest against, letting it take the weight of my pack off my back for a while. I waited for Rob to catch up and he did the same before we both continued south-east. With our heads down, we did the only thing that we could at this point, which was to put one foot in front of the other and to keep on moving. Time takes on its own meaning when you just try to blank out the world and focus on one task, in this case, staying upright.

I have no idea how far or for how long we walked before we came to a railway line which ran perilously close to the top of this high cliff and which surprisingly looked like it was still in use. The line ran to Loftus southbound and Brotton northbound, though in a very roundabout manner. Although the two villages were only a couple of miles apart, the route of the railway doubled this so as to avoid the rather big Warsett Hill which lies between them. I guess it was cheaper to go around than to build a tunnel, though this might prove to have been a false economy with the cliffs looking like they are rapidly eroding and getting closer and closer to the lines. Don't worry about falling off there one day though, as this line is only open to freight traffic, chiefly the nearby Boulby Mine, and passenger trains are not allowed, in case they plummet over the cliff presumably.

The mine, incidentally, appears boring at first glance, but dig a bit deeper, if you pardon the pun, and it's a place I would love to visit. Both the UK Centre for Astrobiology and the European Space Agency send their best geeks down to around 3,600 feet underground to conduct experiments which might help us find out whether or not organisms can survive in salt-rich environments, which they justifiably believe also exist in caves on alien worlds.

They are also busy trying to look for WIMPS, which are not, in fact, small Yorkshire people such as me, but weakly interacting massive particles, or in plain English, the primary candidate for dark matter, thought by some to make up 85% of the total matter in the universe. It must be said, however, that there are increasing calls by others saying that it may not exist at all, so it might ultimately prove to be a fruitless search. On closer inspection of the mine though, there are several experiments currently looking into or for dark matter, all with impressive acronyms, such as ZEPLIN, DRIFT and SKY, which leads me to ask how much time these boffins take thinking of them, which is probably not much come to think of it.

The most impressive experiment though involves the low-pressure negative ion time projection chamber, which they could have christened NITPIC but for some reason, chose not to. Anyway, I have no idea for definite what it is, but I want in, as I reckon it is actually a time machine, even if they say it isn't. Well, they would say that, wouldn't they?

Going back to Brotton, not literally, of course, we've walked enough miles without adding some on, this is the place that we have to thank for the figure that sits on the front of almost every Rolls-Royce. Go out and check yours. Known as the Spirit of Ecstasy, Brotton is the birthplace of its creator, Charles Sykes. He had been commissioned by Lord Montagu of Beaulieu to produce a sculpture for the front of his own roller, who advised Sykes to use Eleanor Velasco Thornton as his model, with whom Lord Montagu was having a torrid affair. As mentioned, the result now sits on the front of almost every car Rolls-Royce ever made, but Montagu also had his own unique and somewhat appropriate variant made.

The Silver Lady, as it is alternately known, generally shows a woman leaning forward with what looks like wings behind her and with her arms outstretched, though the wings are in fact her clothes billowing in the wind. Imagine the downhill skiing position, but without the skis, it looks something like that. Montagu's version though shows the lady with a forefinger to her lips, and is called *The Whisper*, more or less suggesting that everyone should shut the hell up about his fancy woman, not just because of their secret affair, however, but because of her lowly social status. She had been born Nelly Thornton, and simply made up Eleanor Velasco to make herself sound posh.

Interestingly, Henry Royce, the big boss, hated it and refused to drive any vehicle that had one fitted, saying it obscured the driver's view and was generally a bit naff. He made sure that it was only to be listed as an optional extra, but the company started putting it on more or less all of their cars anyway, primarily to stop other people putting even naffer pieces of tat on them, which had become a bit of a craze.

Sykes lived to the grand old age of seventy-five, but Eleanor died very young in 1915, aged just 35. She had been on her way to India with Montagu for a long dirty weekend when the ship they were on, the SS Persia, was torpedoed in the Mediterranean, just south of Crete. Montagu mysteriously survived, of course, which leads me to think that women and children first was nothing but a saying. The Persia was sunk by a German submarine, U-38, which got me all excited, and while this may sound odd, please let me explain.

In my last book, *54 Degrees North*, I wrote about a submarine that had been particularly active and rather successful, the captain of which then transferred to another submarine and came up here to do a fair bit of damage. That submarine also had the identification number of 38, but it turns out they were different vessels. That one was UB-38, a subtle but distinct difference meaning that it was of a different design, and if the Germans were deliberately trying to confuse the British by doing this, well, they got me.

On a final note, Eleanor left all of her possessions to her sister, including one of the original models of the Spirit of Ecstasy, which was later nicked during a burglary at her house. It must be out there somewhere, so check your shed now, because you never know.

Next to the railway line, we came across a nice piece of art, which was basically a giant charm bracelet, and included giant charms in the shape of a cat and a mermaid, among other things. I think it was meant to clang in the wind and make a sound, but it was positively partying today.

After another mile and a half, the path finally descended into Skinningrove, which at least gave us some shelter even if just for a short while. There is not a lot here, but just over half a mile away is Loftus, home to Lewis Hunton. Unless you're into rock, and I don't mean music, you have probably never heard of him. He lived a short but fruitful life before dying prematurely aged only 23 years of age while on a trip to France. It is Hunton who gave science the idea that the surface of the earth, when excavated, could be divided into layers or strata, and therefore help us guess how old things like fossils may be. He probably got the idea from nearby Boulby Cliff, just a bit further along on our journey, where it is pretty easy to see this without digging a really deep hole. There is a small information board here that tells you all about Hunton, so I guess they must be rightly proud of him, and so they should be, and it also describes the rocks around here as fossiliferous, which is a great word that I have never heard before but one that I intend to use as much as I can for the rest of my life.

We followed a sandy beach for a while before going through a gap in the concrete jetty and into the village itself. It was deserted today, as was everywhere apparently, but we were accompanied by a rogue beach ball for a few hundred yards until it blew off ahead of us. At some point, an elderly granny must have managed to catch it and emerged from around a corner with it, asking if it was ours, as if. This made us laugh though, and when she realized what she had asked us, and seeing our huge backpacks, she saw the funny side too.

Seeing the woman catch the ball, I was reminded of the story of the oarfish that was caught here a while back in 2003, which even made the national news. Val Fletcher, a local resident and amateur fisherwoman, caught one of the beasts while night fishing here. Imagine a giant prehistoric eel, or maybe and probably Nessie, and you will have the rough idea. They can grow up to 50 feet long and are the longest bony fish in the sea. They usually live in much warmer and deeper waters, so maybe it was lost or on holiday, who knows. Anyway, reel it in she did, and got her five minutes of fame. The Natural History Museum wanted to preserve the fishy specimen and add it to their permanent collection, but in true Yorkshire style, Val had already chopped it into pieces and served it up with chips for herself along with half of Skinningrove.

Soon enough, after crossing a bridge and leaving the hamlet behind, the path climbed back up again, and once more into the winds. The route became a bit more undulating here and required a lot more effort as a result. We seemed to be rising higher and higher, which I figured must mean we were getting near to Boulby, which is one of the highest places on the coastline around here. On the way up, I asked a group of hikers coming down from the top if there was perhaps a bench up there, or maybe a defibrillator or something. We passed the top at some point though it is hard to say when because of the poor visibility, which also meant that we missed the sight that so inspired Lewis Hunton. This cliff actually turned out to be the highest on the east coast of England, at around 666 feet and is, therefore, a bit of a devil. Obviously, after this, you would expect the path to start dropping, as it did, although in a haphazard sort of fashion.

The path had definitely begun to descend as we neared Staithes though, and the muddy track soon joined what was a very nice path, though it felt immediately hard on the feet as we arrived at the edge of the village. Some of the route had been diverted due to the original path having gone for a bit of a swim, but the replacement was excellent.

A small footbridge took us into the village proper, and we found shelter opposite the Royal George under a gazebo that a café had put up. The cafe was closed, but we still took advantage of their bench to have a rest for a while. A few moments after we sat down, a maintenance man came out and began to talk to us. Telling him that we were doing the Cleveland Way, he said that he himself had done it around fifty years ago, more or less as it opened in 1969, which means he must have been one of the first people to complete it. He had come out to try to fix a section of fence that was flapping about dangerously in the strong winds. He tried decorator's tape, which lasted about 5 seconds, so Rob gave him some electrical tape that he had in his backpack. I guess that explained at least some of the so-called essential weight in his bag, but Rob said he had it in case he needed to repair boots or anything else that broke along the way, such as his legs or my neck. Rob used to be a scout, and I think he secretly still is, and of course, their motto is to *be prepared*. Sometimes I think his bag was inspired by Mary Poppins, seeing some of the stuff that comes out of it.

I mentioned before that Staithes was one of the places that Captain Cook spent a part of his life in. He came here as an apprentice to the brother of his dad's boss, a man called James Sanderson, and spent eighteen months here learning to be a draper and living in the shop under the counter, not quite like Harry Potter but nearly. Maybe Sanderson saw something in Cook, as he would later recommend him as an apprentice to his friend John Walker in Whitby, or maybe he just wanted rid of him because he was a terrible draper. Either way, that is where Cook went next, and where we will eventually follow.

The rain was still persisting it down and looked to have set in for the rest of the day, which dampened our spirits considerably, but rest over, we carried on regardless. We passed the Cod and Lobster, which was right on the seafront and has often taken the brunt of winter storms here. In 1953, the front of the pub was washed away and had to be rebuilt, and they now have a back door, just in case. None of the houses around here have street numbers but instead have quaint old names, often in salute of fishing boats. The Royal Mail at one point tried to get everyone to number their houses instead, but the townspeople basically told them to get stuffed, so they gave up.

Following the jumble of narrow streets, the path eventually led up a hill, of course, at the top of which we found several dozen steps once again taking us up into the clouds. Once at the top, however, the path settled off again, and after a brief rest, we carried on up a gentle incline. It flattened out at the top and Rob went ahead at a good pace. I saw a young man stood uncomfortably close to the edge and for one minute wondered if he was going to jump, but I think he was just taking a selfie.

As I neared him, he turned around and asked me where I was going. He said he was from Beverley, just a few miles from where I lived, and it always amazes me how you can travel far and wide and bump into people from the next street or town. Perhaps this was more likely this year, what with several people choosing, and by choosing, I mean forced, to take a holiday within the United Kingdom. Anyway, he knew the area well and suggested a good campsite at a waterfall called Hayburn Wyke. He was called Mark and told me he had camped there once or twice himself, including when he did the Cleveland Way a couple of years back. I thanked him and made a mental note of the name just in case it turned out that we would be stopping somewhere in that area, which I thought unlikely.

Port Mulgrave was soon upon us, where we saw that some interesting shacks had been built far below us on the rocks. There was not much else there, as the Royal Engineers had done a pretty good job of blowing up anything that was left during the Second World War to thwart any possible plans the Germans might have to land at this godforsaken place. I had been told that this is the only Port along the Yorkshire coast. I know, I know, Hull is a port, but what I mean is that it is the only place in Yorkshire that is actually called Port this or that, which is odd because you would expect there to be a few, but there aren't. We passed through in no time at all, with our next, and possibly final destination for the day being Runswick Bay, just a mile or two further along.

We had decided that if we could get that far today, then that would be enough, and we would camp at the first available and suitable spot. The path took a turn inland before going into the village itself, which involved a very steep path down to the beach and car park, going past the Cliffemount Hotel. We had been tempted to take the road which seemed a bit more direct, but this was steeper still and would have required mountaineering gear. Two guys came out and accompanied us down the hill, asking if we were camping. They then told us about a possible location for a good campsite, which they said was behind the yacht club, and pointed across the bay to a blue building in the distance. As we were talking, their ever so cute dog decided to do a giant dump right in front of me. Thanking them, not for the dump obviously, but for the directions, we moved on intending to go and check out this potential campsite, but as we got to the club, a 4x4 pulled up, and some people got out, so we decided to move on.

We passed lots of holes in the cliffs, which I had heard of and read about, but had never seen. They are called Hob Holes, and inside each one is supposed to live a Hobgoblin, which happens to be our favourite beer. Hobgoblins were supposed to be cheeky little sprites that might help you out, but if you annoyed them, they would turn on you and make your life hell. They are often portrayed as being very small and wearing scruffy clothes and shaggy hair, which brings to mind our good friend Chris, and in some accounts, they were actually seen while naked, which brings us straight back to Chris. Some say that they also had healing powers, particularly when it came to children, and in days gone by, parents would bring children who were suffering from whooping cough to these caves, recite a poem in a Yorkshire accent, and hope for a miracle.

The caves are small but big enough to go into, and probably quite dangerous, which just makes it exciting when you do go in one, so it is probably a good idea to send the kids in first. They are actually the result of jet mining many decades ago even though they look like they might have been formed naturally. I went into the largest one I saw but didn't stay long, quickly ruling it out as a place to spend the night, so we moved on.

Our next camping option was hopefully at the top of the cliff in a small wood, but after a rigorous ascent, with a lot of puffing and panting, we got to the top to find it wholly unsuitable. I walked ahead to try and scout out a campsite as Robin was having ankle problems, and I soon came across the old railway line. Right at the point where the path joined the line sat a small bench, in front of which was a tiny patch of grass that looked just about the right size for our tent. There were no cowpats here, no dangerous animals to gobble us up in the night, and I could see no obvious reason not to camp here although it was a bit exposed and just a trifle windy. I went back to the path and attracted Rob's attention, and when he joined me, we both agreed that this was the place to stop.

We sat for a while on the bench just getting our breath back. The rain had eased off, and the wind had died down considerably, but it was still a bit wild. Once we got the tent up, though, we were confident of a good night's sleep, as in our current state, there was once again little that could keep us awake, certainly not a bit of wind.

Suitably rested, we got the bits out for the tent and laid it on the ground, whereupon it all nearly blew away. Grabbing it just before it disappeared forever, which would surely end this walk, we regained control and started to put the poles through it. We just about had it set up when a strong gust blew up and ripped it away from us once again. It flattened out in the air, almost becoming a kite, and whipped Robin across the face.

I grabbed it, pulled it down, and laid on it, confident that my weight would now finally come in useful for something, and congratulating myself on all those years of eating chocolate and biscuits. After trying once again to stake it down and seeing the wind almost rip it away from us, we came to the conclusion that this was perhaps not the best spot to make camp tonight. We had been beaten, we had failed, and we had only one option, to pack the tent away and move on, hopefully to a five-star hotel.

Packing it up as best as we could, we trudged on along the railway line, which ran parallel to the path along the clifftop, as we figured that if we could get just a little bit further away from the coast, we would have a better chance of finding a sheltered spot for the tent though zero chance of finding a hotel. There were few options, with the occasional spot being too small or too bumpy, and as we neared Kettleness, we feared we would be walking a bit further still to find a suitable spot. Wild camping, which is technically illegal in most of England, is perhaps somewhat tolerated to a point. The general rule is to arrive late, just before darkness, and to pack up and leave early, shortly after first light. Leave no trace is also the slogan used by all responsible wild campers, as well as generally making sure you do not camp anywhere silly, such as in Jeremy Clarkson's back garden or on a helipad. It is common sense really, which is why I thought that once we were near

Kettleness, we would not be able to find anywhere suitable.

Robin, however, had managed to spot a little gem of a place. Nestled just off the railway line, in a small clearing in between some trees, was a patch of grass that was the perfect size for us and our small tent. There was a house nearby, but it was out of sight, and as it was beginning to get dark, we decided we had no option but to plonk down here. The little spot was quite well shielded from the weather, too, and when we got the tent out, we had no problems with the wind and soon had it up. In no time at all, we were inside, with the kettle on and brewing our nightly coffee with a little something in it. Once again, the universe was in perfect balance.

Darkness came pretty quickly. Inside the tent, though, we had a light on and were chatting about the days walk while we had a little bit of supper in the form of our various snacks. Before I went to sleep, I stepped outside to try to get enough signal to send my wife a text, and as I was doing so, a car drove past on the little track. Half a minute later, another one went past, then another and finally one more. This was a puzzle as we had seen nothing along the track, so I presumed there was either a rave going on, to which we were not invited, or maybe someone was going to do a spot of hunting. Getting back into the tent, we were both quickly pretty much asleep, and I did not hear the cars on their return journey. At some point, it got a bit windy once again, and I don't mean outside. I decided there and then that Rob was forevermore banned from eating jerky with no exceptions.

It was another night of broken sleep, especially as the wind picked up again and bellowed through the trees above our heads for most of the night. I remember thinking, as I drifted off to sleep, that if the wind did blow a tree down on us, it would be a merciful and swift ending to a fabulous walk, though not necessarily the one we had envisaged.

CHAPTER 6
Kettleness to Cloughton

I awoke the next morning to the sound of Robin rustling out of his sleeping bag. He told me we had slept in and that it was almost a quarter to seven. I laid there for a minute enjoying the last few moments of warmth before I reluctantly dragged myself out too, and started to pack my gear. We brewed a coffee and shared a couple of breakfast bars, and by 7.30 am, we were up and walking. Funnily enough, the building that we had slept near to turned out to be a scout camp, with some fine grass available for pitching tents, had we had a closer look last night. I could only guess that scouting activities were still suspended due to the pandemic, as there were no signs of life at the camp, not even any vehicles parked up there. I imagine we could have easily camped there without upsetting anyone had we chosen to, which is just typical, as we always seem to find a decent campsite twelve hours too late.

We ambled through Kettleness back towards the sea and the path and headed south towards Sandsend. The going was pretty easy, with a nice wide track to follow that was very well maintained, and at this early hour, we had it to ourselves. This was the old railway line, and we caught a glimpse of the southern end of the old Sandsend Tunnel which is almost a mile long. I would like to come back one day to have a look inside as I am told that some of the air shafts have other tunnels going off horizontally towards the cliffs and the sea, which were used for dumping excavated earth straight into the water below.

Further along, there were some spectacular Alum deposits on our left, this area being a major source of the stuff up until just over a hundred years ago. It was used in the tanning industry and was relatively easy to get out of the ground in these parts, but more of that later. The landscape that has been left today is basically a result of that industry, though. Although it is man-made and quite stark, it is still incredibly beautiful and quite impressive, especially when compared to the lush greenery that is everywhere else.

Sandsend itself was also very nice in its way. The sand stretched before us from where the car park was at the north end, which I guess is where the rather original name came from, and despite the early hour, the place was buzzing. The car park was already half full with surfers prepping for a day of fun, and fishermen were gathering their tackle to go and land the big one. Rob made use of the facilities in the car park while I sat on a bench watching the world go by. I repacked my rucksack as it felt a bit out of balance, as did I after all these miles. The sun was coming out, and it glistened on the water far out to sea, almost to the point of blinding you if you looked at it for too long, and although the weather looked far more promising than yesterday, there were still some threatening looking clouds moving in from the north. As we moved off, I almost left my sleeping bag behind and only grabbed it because Rob noticed it on the bench.

We departed from the path for a while, deciding instead to walk on the sand just for a change of scenery. This wasn't necessarily easier, it was just more enjoyable, but almost immediately Robin cockled over on his ankle. His sticks saved him once again, and we moved up the beach towards the flatter and more compressed sand. The tide was well and truly out so we figured we could walk all the way to Whitby along the beach if we wanted to, which was only around two and a half miles away. The odd dog walker said good morning to us, but other than that we had the beach to ourselves.

Whitby Abbey stood proudly on the hill before us, and slowly, ever so slowly, it seemed to be getting nearer. After a mile or so, we came across a row of traditional British beach huts, but these were superior to others we had seen in that they were all brightly painted, each one being a random colour of the rainbow, and the whole thing looked fantastic in the early morning sunlight. Here, however, Robin stumbled again, and although his sticks stopped him going over completely, I could see from the look on his face that he had either hurt himself really bad, or he needed the loo. Being the trooper that he is though, he carried on regardless, and by the time we arrived in Whitby, he seemed to have walked it off.

We walked up the ramp that led to the town and were surprised at the hustle and bustle that greeted us at the top, despite the early hour. Families with children wandered aimlessly, dog walkers were everywhere, and the noise of traffic, seagulls and the people themselves offered an amazing contrast to the serenity of the beach. Signs adorned walls everywhere, seemingly warning of the risk of death, or even worse, a £1000 fine, should you dare give a chip to a gull, which I thought a bit over the top. We were soon near the bridge, where we intended to cross the River Esk and climb the 199 steps up to the Abbey. First, though, we stopped for a rest, and Robin went off in search of water as we were running a little bit low. He returned some minutes later, mission accomplished and said that the cafe owner had told him that a lot of holidaymakers had gone home early due to the poor weather of the previous day. Although I could understand why they might have done this, I still thought it was a shame, as today was looking really quite promising.

Off we went, through the town, and halfway across the bridge, we noticed that a one-way system was in operation to help with social distancing, and of course, we were going the wrong way. We immediately stopped and waited for the traffic to clear so we could cross to the right side, but not before a woman coming the other way loudly sounded her obvious displeasure at having to pass two smelly backpackers who had failed their one and only job, which was to read a sign. I gave her my best evil look, which I had been practising for many years, but I fear I am still at the stage where it makes me look like a constipated hippo. As for the woman, I can only describe her as being rude in behaviour and sluttish.

Now on the right side of the path, we both became immediately annoyed by all of the people going the wrong way. I mean, they only had one job, which was to read a sign, for goodness sake. It must be noted here that it is a habit of intelligent human beings to be easily annoyed by those around them, but saying nothing in order to avoid a pointless argument, so by virtue of saying nothing, I figured I must be of big brain.

Turning off into the labyrinth of little side streets that pass for the town centre, the crowds became denser and it seemed that everyone had had the same idea, which was to get out early and beat the crowds. I passed another little café where the girl on the door was telling prospective customers that it was cash only and grumbled to Rob about them robbing the taxpayer and how we, ultimately, will have to foot the bill.

I had developed a theory, you see. What I suspected these cafes were doing was this. The government had introduced the eat out to help out scheme which promised heavily discounted food on a Monday, Tuesday or Wednesday. Businesses sold their food at half price and could claim up to £10 per customer back from the government. If they insisted on cash on the other days of the week, which means Thursday to Sunday, they could then put this through the books on, say, the Monday, or whichever day they chose. So, if they took £2000 in cash between Thursday and Sunday, by putting it through as a transaction on that Monday, they could instantly turn it into £4000. Simples. Unethical, dishonest and thieves they would be, but simples it is, as my good friend Yoda would say.

There was no way I was going to give any of my hard-earned cash to such unscrupulous peoples, so we moved on. Rounding a corner, we were at the steps that led up to the abbey, but took a moment to rest, as they looked quite imposing from down here. I began my traipse up, and to be fair, I soon found myself more or less halfway with Rob not far behind. I came across one of the benches that dotted the steps and stopped to take a breath. A lady sat on it, clearly puffed out just like me, and she was giving her dog a little treat.

I had great pleasure in telling her that these

benches were not originally intended for unfit tourists, but were, in fact, resting points where mourners would put down coffins so they could avoid having a heart attack as they carried it up for the service and subsequent burial at the top. I told her that Count Dracula had also sprinted up these steps, although while in the guise of a wolf, in Bram Stoker's famous novel Dracula, which has very well-known links to the town and owes itself at least partly to this place. She looked quite alarmed at all this, to be honest. I finished by suggesting she might not want to spend too long there.

It would be remiss of me to leave Whitby without mentioning a little bit more about Dracula, as the place relies heavily on drawing tourists in nowadays mainly because of this. Stoker had first become familiar with Whitby when he used to come here on holiday as a child, and I guess the place stuck with him into adulthood. The abbey is probably the clincher for the deal, though, its ruins standing spookily on the headland above the town, and is best viewed on a dark misty night.

The book was originally called *The Dead Un-Dead* with Dracula himself being based on Vlad the Impaler, and it is hard to decide who the best Dracula character ever was. Stoker had sort of based Dracula on a colleague of his, a guy called Henry Irving, who was said to embody Dracula's mannerisms and who was therefore probably ace to meet in person. I am torn between Bela Lugosi and Christopher Lee for the best portrayal of the Count, and it has to be said that without Stoker's original creation, we would not have such modern classics as Buffy the Vampire Slayer or Sesame Street's The Count, and certainly no Goth weekend, for which Whitby is famous. How would civilization cope without all that, I wondered.

Rob had gone well ahead of me by now as I had spent a good few minutes gabbing, so I carried on step by step, avoiding looking up so as to not see how far was left. I had been trying to count the steps to see if there really were 199, but when I spoke to the dog lady, I had lost count and had no intention of going back down and starting again.

I finally reached the top and found Robin slumped on a bench in front of the church, being administered with medical assistance, and I suspected it would be more humane to put him out of his misery instead. I joined him for a much-appreciated rest and thought of investing in a hoverboard or something for these hills. We could clearly see the ruins of the abbey, which was where most of the tourists seemed to be going, though we were heading along the cliff top in the opposite direction, but not until we had shared half a bar of Kendal mint cake. The view of the harbour was also great, and we could easily make out the arch made of whale bones just across the far side of the River Esk, and close by it was the Captain Cook Memorial. The Esk is the only major river we will cross on this coastal section of the walk, as all of the other rivers around here find their way to the sea through either the Humber to the south or the Tees to the north, which is probably because of the relatively high land that most of the coast is composed of. Out to sea, minke whales are known to make a star appearance between August and October, but there was no sign today, unfortunately.

We had once again caught up with Captain Cook, who had moved from Staithes to Whitby and joined a shipping firm as a trainee. Here he lived in the attic of his boss, John Walker, on Grape Lane. Luckily, nobody has, as yet, dismantled this house brick by brick and shipped it to Australia, so it is now a museum all about Cook and Cookie-related things.

Grape lane was previously known as Grope Lane, by the way, and the powers that be will tell you that it was once a dark passage that you had to grope your way through, but don't you believe a word of it. As with many streets that had this name, there is the probability that this is where you would come on a night for a bit of fun, nudge nudge, wink wink.

Whitby is also where two of Cook's most famous ships would later be built, the *Resolution* and the *Endeavour*. The Endeavour was the ship Cook took on his first voyage of discovery, becoming the first ship to reach the east coast of Australia. During this voyage, he also claimed for the crown various islands including Bora Bora, much to the bemusement of the locals. The Resolution took part in Cook's second voyage and became one of the first ships known to have crossed into the Antarctic Circle, and this journey is regarded by some as one of the greatest voyages of all time.

His third and final voyage, once again in the Resolution, took him ultimately to Hawaii, where after an initial friendship with the locals, things went drastically wrong. They nicked one of the small boats from Cook's ship, which did not please him, to say the least. He then went ashore to arrest their king, which in retrospect was perhaps not the best idea, and a fight ensued. Contemporary accounts tell of a brave Cook dying after being stabbed in the back yet ordering his troops not to fire, but in reality, he was involved in a bitter fight to the death and was finally stabbed in the neck, according to a first-hand account by the ship's carpenter.

That is the last that anyone heard of Cook, and indeed it is the last that we will hear of him, as his story stops in Whitby. Incidentally, it is possible that the Endeavour, up until now thought to be lost forever, has recently been found a few fathoms deep somewhere off the coast of Rhode Island, so watch this space.

Less well known than Cook was a chap called William Scoresby, and there is also a statue of him to be found here. There are actually two Williams, and they are father and son, both sailing out of Whitby at some point in their lives. Starting with Scoresby senior, it was this bright spark who came up with the idea of the crow's nest in 1807, which is of course that barrel-like thing at the top of many a ship's masts, another fine Yorkshire invention. You will see a statue commemorating this next to the harbour just in front of the train station. He probably invented it so he could kill more whales, him being the most successful whale hunter ever, apparently, bagging 533 in his life. I had always thought the crow's nest was ancient though, and had imagined them on many an ancient galleon, so I was quite surprised to find that it was only invented around 200 years or so ago.

Scoresby junior was famous for different reasons, chiefly having a pretty good reputation as an arctic explorer. He held the record for having travelled furthest north for a good while and was one of the first people to introduce us to the fact that every snowflake that ever fell is unique. By the way, when I was trying to read up to figure out whether all snowflakes really are unique (probably, but only just) I found out that there are roughly one billion snowflakes in a pile of snow which is one-foot square. I'll check in winter and get back to you. I also tried to find out why snowflakes are symmetrical, which is something to do with crystallization, but I'll be honest with you, the science went beyond me like a bullet train.

You may have noticed the pier sticking itself out into the North Sea here, and be wondering why I said earlier that Saltburn had the only pier in Yorkshire. Well, when we talk of piers, we are talking of pleasure piers, and you may have noticed that the one in Whitby is totally different, being very narrow and serving a purpose, rather than purely something for bored tourists to stroll up and down and stick their money into slot machines and stuff their faces with sticks of rock and candy floss. So, there you go.

I always like to try and find out something about a place which is perhaps not all that well known, and there is such a fact to be discovered about Whitby. Everyone knows that the sun rises in the east and sets in the west, so if you want to watch a sunrise in England, you come to the east coast, and if you want to watch a sunset, you go to the west coast. Sounds simple enough. But Whitby is an oddity where you can actually watch both a sunrise and a sunset from the same place, though only at certain times of the year. This is because the coastline here runs more or less east to west and faces due north, which means that from around mid-May to late July, this anomaly becomes possible. You do, however, have to get a clear evening to be able to do this, so good luck with that. There is only one other place on the east coast where this is possible, apparently, and that is in and near to Cromer in Norfolk.

Before we go, I want to share one last thing about Whitby with you. Many, many moons ago, when I was a lad, so to speak, a very youthful looking Mick Hucknall, who is, of course, the rock god front-man of Simply Red, filmed a video here to go with his song *Holding Back the Years*. If you watch it, it is more or less a tour around the entire town as it looked way back in 1985, and of course, much of it hasn't changed. In real life, Hucknall was sadly estranged from his mum for a very long time, and it is that experience which inspired this most poignant song, which makes the words all the more meaningful. Watch the video and see if you can figure out which room he was in, I think I have.

Finally leaving Whitby behind, and following the cliff path once again, it quickly became apparent that we had come the wrong way when we met a stone wall and could go no further. We were not the only ones to have been caught out here, though. The half-dozen or so people in front of us had all decided to hop over the wall with the help of a well-placed stone in the ground, so we decided to do the same, and joined the queue. Yes, there really was a queue; us Brits love to queue. I considered keeping my pack on but quickly realized that I would probably end up on the floor in a position something similar to a tortoise stuck on its back if I did so. Backpacks off, a young man offered to help us get them over the wall, and I jokingly told him not to run off with them. Unless he had a kinky fetish for smelly socks, there was probably not a lot in there for him, it had to be said.

The path that led us out of Whitby was fairly level though a little narrow in places. We passed a large field that looked like it was experiencing the back end of a festival, which was odd considering the current global killer pandemic doing the rounds. There were caravans everywhere, along with a portable toilet block and several power generators, though I could not think what event might have been happening due to the current situation and the regulations and difficulties that came with it.

Far below us on the rocks, I could see a shipwreck of one kind or another. I suspected that this was all that was left of the MV Creteblock, an unusual name for a ship until you find out that it was made of concrete block. It is hard to imagine a ship made of concrete faring pretty well, and you could argue that the proof of this is down there right before you. But the ship, and many like it, actually sailed pretty well. They were common by the end of the First World War when steel was being saved to build battleships, and this one only ended up here when it had fulfilled its purpose and was being towed out to sea to be sunk, but hit these rocks after the towing line snapped.

At this point, I noticed that my little toe was giving me trouble and I suspected a blister had burst, so I suggested to Rob that we stop as soon as there was something to sit on. Luckily, after a mile or two, we came to the impressive old foghorn station, where some entrepreneurial individual had set up a coffee shop. We stopped, well, we had to, as, in these difficult times, it is even more crucial than ever to support struggling local businesses. Plus, we were knackered, and I had that blister to sort out. Rob went to get us a coffee while I took off my shoe and peeled back my sock. I got a couple of funny looks from people who understandably did not want to see this, but I had moved beyond the point of caring. It did not actually look too bad, and the blister plaster that I had put on the night before was still in place. This being the case, I had no option but to just leave it and carry on and could not really understand why it had suddenly decided to start giving me so much hassle.

We got talking to three guys on the next table who were also doing the Cleveland Way, though in the opposite direction to us, and they told us that this was their third day. They were not carrying large backpacks; instead, they were having them shipped along from hotel to hotel, so were clearly enjoying a leisurely walk, and I don't blame them one bit. But it dawned on me that what they had taken two and a half days to do without heavy packs, we were going to do in one and a half days complete with heavy packs. This unsettled me for a while until I reminded myself that I had no doubt whatsoever that we could finish this now, bar some unfortunate event such as being squashed by a falling grand piano or kidnapped by radical vegans with a revolutionary and anti-jerky agenda. So, with a hot coffee in our belly, we moved on, and now had the end in sight, in our minds at least.

This part of the walk was uneventful; the further we got from Whitby, the fewer people we saw. A sign pointed towards a side trail and the village of Hawsker, after which the monotony continued, interrupted only by the occasional flight of steps that meant a few moments of breathlessness. The monotony did not mean boring as such, as the views across this stretch were just as beautiful as the rest. It has got to be said, though, that at some point you can start to become desensitized to beauty, and you have to remind yourself how lucky you are to be out here enjoying this, which I certainly was, apart from the blisters and the on-off rain and the heavy pack of course.

Eventually, and not a minute too soon, Robin Hood's Bay started to come into view. Tantalizing glimpses of boats on the beach, followed by the first sight of houses, eventually gave way to a full-on view of the village, looking splendid and very picturesque in the morning sun. The tide was still out, and tiny figures dotted the landscape below us though it was impossible to pick out any detail.

Robin Hood's Bay was said to have been a haven for smugglers and looking down on the cascade of cottages and narrow alleyways before us, it was easy to see why. The good view of both the town and the sea made spots such as where I stood now ideal lookout points used to warn of any coming revenue men though I suspect nowadays it is more commonly used for selfies. There were also supposed to be lots of Scooby-Doo type tunnels and secret passages between and under the houses, which would be awesome if true. So, if your gran disappears while leaning against a wall in the Laurel Inn or Ye Dolphin, you know where she has probably gone.

I had read that at one point in the 18th century, 80% of all tea drunk in the country was drunk illegally, which brings to mind illicit but comical night time meetings with the sole intention of consuming the good stuff. The smuggling of silk and tobacco was also rife, and while the risks were high, with the death sentence certainly possible if caught, the rewards were equally high. Down by the harbour, there is what was supposed to be one of the old smugglers' tunnels, but to me, it looks just like an old sewer if I am brutally honest. Finally, akin to Saltburn, ladies here were also said to be wandering around the town with all sorts of things shoved into their bras and knickers, as the customs men would never check them, which makes me think that ladies was, perhaps, not quite the right word.

We passed through a couple of gates, which was quite challenging as they were not designed for chubby blokes with backpacks, and then followed a snicket with high hedges on either side, finally coming out at some houses on the outskirts of the town. The path ran right through the middle of some gardens, and many *private property* signs dotted perfectly manicured patches of grass, which would have made great campsites.

Emerging onto a bustling road next to a car park was quite a culture shock, and we saw more people gathered in one place than we had seen at any other point along the walk, or indeed for the last six months. The Grosvenor Hotel could have been our first port of call had all the tables not been occupied already, so we decided to head down into the town and grab some fish and chips as well as a drink from somewhere else. The road became incredibly steep here, and I had visions of Rob going over again, but luckily, he didn't, and we made good progress. Halfway down, though, we were halted when Rob saw someone he knew, another Paul, and a conversation began. Coincidentally, it was this guy's birthday, and he was choosing to spend it here of all places, which was a fine choice, and one that had been made by half of Yorkshire, apparently.

As we descended, the crowds did not thin out at all, in fact, if anything, it got more crowded. There were not many places to eat, and what few there were all seemed to have long queues. We got to the bottom, next to the harbour, and found somewhere to sit, and surveyed the scene. It was absolutely rammed with people down here, and I had a slight feeling of unease.

I had been here many times, most recently when we had completed the Coast to Coast Walk, which finishes here. The Bay Hotel, where there is a large and well-photographed sign announcing the end of the walk, had a queue of perhaps a dozen people waiting for the opportunity to eat, and it did not seem to be moving at all. I found the chip shop after asking a guy who was sat eating his opposite us and told Rob to hold tight while I went to grab some. Unfortunately, this was not meant to be. When I got there, they had an even longer queue, which again was not moving. A man emerged with a bag full of food, and when I asked him how long he had been waiting, he told me just over half an hour. I offered to buy his off him and was only half-joking.

After walking around ten miles or so already today, I was neither prepared nor capable of standing still for that length of time, so I went back to the harbour and gave Rob the bad news. I did still have some jerky and a bit of chocolate in my bag, which we shared while we made our plans for what to do next, but this was little consolation to a big, fat, greasy haddock.

As well as not being willing to stand in a queue for an age in order to get some food, I was also not willing to listen to the guy that had now approached me trying to sell me a joke book. I had been watching him fleece passing tourists with a very hard sell approach and was very much in their faces. He did not reckon on me though and my independent, assertive nature, and I don't think he realised who he was dealing with. He was not local, I'm guessing South Yorkshire somewhere, possibly Wakefield, as he had quite a strong twang. Anyway, I'm not too sure what happened, but I quite enjoyed reading my new purchase, although it was a bit steep at five pounds.

Looking at the map, Boggle Hole was just over the hill, maybe a mile or two away. I had been there with my dad quite recently and knew that there was a Youth Hostel there complete with facilities and more importantly, a café. Rob was happy with this, so after a brief interlude, we bade farewell to a very crowded Robin Hood's Bay and headed south. Unfortunately, after a five-minute walk, we were heading back towards the town, having gone the wrong way.

Course corrected, we now headed up a steep hill, obviously and as always, and eventually joined a narrow and constrained little path. Luckily, nobody was coming the other way, as the path, overgrown at this time of year, did not provide enough room to allow people with ridiculous rucksacks to pass mere mortals with any kind of social distancing. I got ahead again, and waited at a bench, talking to an elderly couple who told me they were out for a stroll. I told them that we, too, were out for a stroll, and wondered about the distance to and quality of food at Boggle hole. What they said didn't exactly enthuse me with optimism, but on we plodded, finally reaching the place only to find it too, crowded with people.

There were no tables free, but at this point, we didn't care. Dumping our stuff on the floor, I went to order chips and gravy for us both as well as a large coke. The cokes came first, which if they were large, I would not like to, nor probably be able to see a small one. I took these to Rob and went back to wait for the food, which took perhaps ten minutes. As the chips arrived, Rob was motioning something to me, which I translated as get another drink, but this would mean joining another queue once again, so I didn't bother.

It turns out that Rob had moved to a bench, and in the process had spilt our drinks, and only half of one cup remained. I told him to drink it as I was not that bothered, and we both started to scoff our chips. Imagine one of those small ice-creams that come in a cardboard tub at the cinema and cost a fortune. That was what our chips were in, which was a bit of a disappointment, and they did not last long at all. Still, they filled a gap.

Boggle Hole itself was a nice little place, though there was nothing there. If I remembered correctly, you could not even drive down here, but had to park your car a mile or so away at the top of the hill and walk down, which was why I was surprised it was so busy.

With no reason to stay, and wanting to get some extra miles in today, we put our packs back on and continued on our way. Every time we stopped walking, we found we were seizing up a little, and the longer we stopped for, the worse it seemed to become. We had stopped for a good half hour here, which partly explains why it was so difficult to get going again. Obviously, the path went straight up a hill again, and although it was sort of gentle at first, it soon became much steeper. A series up pointless ups and downs followed, and after every one, we had to stop and get a breath.

Robin and I spent much of the next section walking separately, alternating with who was in front from time to time. A couple of showers threatened us but didn't really get us wet, after which the sun shone intently. I walked for a bit with two ladies, mother and daughter, who were up here for the day to enjoy the countryside. They were very friendly, but I still felt as if I was imposing upon them, so I stopped to wait for Robin to catch up. We were now heading into Ravenscar, which was one of my favourite places around here, and would take a break at the top of what looked like a steep climb. A golf course to our left looked like another possible route popular with walkers but was steeper still. Above this was what looked like a mock Spanish castle, and when Rob arrived, he informed me that it was part of the golf club.

We walked the last stretch into Ravenscar together, and when we got there, Rob grabbed a picnic table, and I went to get us a ridiculously over-priced coke each from the National Trust visitor centre. When I joined him, Arthur from the next table tried to bite me. Arthur turned out to be a dog, and his owner said that he was a nervous one at that, although nervous was perhaps not the word I would use. Vicious, evil and sadistic all spring to mind when something is trying to rip your gizzard out, and nervous is the last adjective that would spring to mind. They were a large and lively family, and very pleasant to talk to as well as being quite funny, apart obviously from their killer dog. One minute they were bickering among themselves, the next they were talking to us. When grandad came back, he had been to the loo he informed us, Arthur tried to rip his gizzard out too, which I found strangely gratifying.

We sipped our cokes slowly, relishing each expensive sip, while we rested and looked at the map to see how far we had come, and were surprised to find that we had covered around 17 miles since leaving Kettleness that morning. We would try to get a bit further on today, maybe up to 20 miles, which would make tomorrow a little bit easier. It would also mean we could meet our families earlier, which would be nice. There was plenty of daylight left, and we both reckoned we still had a little bit more energy left, so putting our packs back on, we plodded on.

We walked through the town of Ravenscar, which is actually not a town. It is somewhat of an oddity, resulting from speculation that failed spectacularly in the late Victorian period. Grand plans were made that would make Peak, as it was going to be called, a holiday resort to rival nearby Whitby and Scarborough. Streets were laid out and given names including Station Road, Cliff Road and Marine Esplanade. A train station was built, sewers were installed, and a few fine houses were constructed, but the tourists never came in what you would call large numbers. The trains that did come struggled to get up the steep gradient of the line and those that did step off the train found this clifftop spot somewhat windswept.

I imagine that the walk to the beach down a 600-foot hill did not exactly sell the idea either. The Victorian dream quickly morphed into a nightmare, and the whole project eventually went off the rails into bankruptcy. It's all still here, though, and is an interesting sight.

Other than the people that live in the few houses though, the vast majority of the occupants have whiskers and fishy breath and are part of the seal colony that can be found on the shore below, which includes both grey and common seals and lots of them and which is also renowned as being very fossiliferous. There, I told you I would use that word again.

We next passed the ruins of what looked like an old industrial site, where through a long, drawn-out and probably quite smelly process, Alum was manufactured in years gone by. Alum was important, as until a synthetic alternative was developed in the late 1800s, it was the best fixative available and allowed textiles to be coloured with the use of vegetable dyes. It was not a simple process, though, and additionally required kelp for potassium, and urine for ammonium. As a key part of this industry, several public urinals were built in my home city of Hull, where it was collected in considerable quantities before being brought here. This quite unlikely story is in point of fact true. When you think about it, they were literally taking the piss, but I can promise you that I am not. I always wondered why my town was blessed with many, very old, public toilets, whereas many other towns were not, and there is the rather surprising answer. On this topic, the Romans also used urine as mouthwash, I kid you not, the filthy beggars.

We carried on and hugged the cliff once again and found that the path was generally dropping now, meaning we were finally reaching the end of this walk. Although my blisters had stopped hurting, in fact, I suspected my little toe had fallen off, my knees and ankles were beginning to give me a bit of trouble. My calf muscle on my right leg seemed solid, which I took as a bad thing, not a good thing, and my ankles and feet were constantly swollen.

Shortly, we passed an old radar station and stopped to have a look. There were some surface buildings left, but I could not see any signs of subterranean buildings. I have been in a couple of these old cold-war bases that turned out to have quite substantial underground elements to them, which are just so interesting to explore. This station was one of many dotted around the coast and utilized the newly invented radar, invented by the British of course, to detect incoming enemy planes. It was eventually replaced by RAF Fylingdales a few miles away and fell into ruin before being rescued by the National Trust. It must be said that Fylingdales, often confusingly called Flyingdales, is not a top-secret base or anything like that, and I never ever flew my drone there ever, and said drone never flew away, never to be seen again at all. Just saying.

Carrying on, we had decided we were now aiming for Hayburn Wyke. This was around 3 miles after Ravenscar and would give us a total of around twenty miles for the day, a very respectable number for incompetent buffoons such as ourselves. If you cast your mind back a bit, Hayburn Wyke was the camping spot that the young lad called Mark had suggested way back in Staithes, and at the time I had thought it unlikely that we would just happen to stop in that area, but here we were. The path was very definitely dropping now as we approached the wood where the falls were hidden, which made it an easier walk than earlier. As we entered the wood, the obligatory steep steps awaited us, but at least we would not have to climb back up the other side until tomorrow.

Descending slowly and carefully, I reached the bottom first and ventured off to the left to find the waterfall and the campsite, following a small path that led around the dense foliage rather than through it. I found the waterfall easily enough but could see no obvious place to pitch a tent. I went off into the trees again to make sure I had not missed anything, but other than a small patch of rocky ground right next to the waterfall itself, there was nowhere obvious that would accommodate us. When Rob reached the bottom of the gully, I beckoned him over to have a look at the spot. I watched him struggle through the plants and bushes, and when he was finally through, I asked him why he had not used the path, pointing to it and laughing. After giving me a grimace and an evil eye, he agreed immediately that it was, well, a crap campsite.

While Rob had a rest, I climbed down to the beach to get a good look at the waterfall. Some teenagers had been building rock columns on the beach, and there were several scattered about, and they all looked quite impressive though they would probably not last long once the tide and weather moved in. I imagined this would be a pretty dangerous place to be during bad weather, and had read that in 1880, during a severe storm, a Swedish ship had broken up offshore, and one of those killed was washed up onto this beach with such force that his head stuck fast into the gaps between the rocks like a cartoon character. A local man, Ed Leadley, with the help of a police officer, had then joined forces to remove the body from this jam, a story which is so strange that it must be true. I mean, who would make that up?

Disheartened, we trudged up the steps, consoling ourselves that at least by getting it out of the way now, we would not have to do this climb first thing in the morning. At the top, the path narrowed, with a barbed-wire fence on the right and a sheer drop on the left, and it just disappeared into the distance with no sign of a suitable campsite. This meant that we had to knock some more distance off before we stopped, but again it would mean less tomorrow, which was about the only positive we could salvage from this. We were both shattered, Rob had had a couple of incidents with his ankle, and all we wanted to do was to stop, eat and sleep.

I ploughed on ahead, hoping to scout out somewhere good to put the tent, and almost considered the side of the path itself. The only thing that put me off was the 200-foot drop immediately adjacent to it, which would make sleepwalking problematic, to say the least. My wife tells me that I do sleepwalk, though I obviously have no memory of ever having done it, so it is definitely something to think about. To my right, a field looks like a good place to pitch a tent, despite having a private property sign attached to the fence.

I have a cunning defence for trespassing on private property, you see, so you might want to make a note of this because it's good. Technically, trespassing is illegal as we all know, but there is a little known exception although it only works on the coast. An act of parliament from 1603 allows huers and baulkers to pretty much go where they want along the shoreline. What is a huer or a baulker you ask? Well, they would stand on the clifftops and direct fishing boats to where the fishes were, and therefore needed access to all of the coast. I'm pretty sure it's still valid, and I keep hoping to get stopped so I can try it out, but as yet I never have been. Annoyingly, however, the fence is topped with barbed wire, which rules it out anyway, as Rob and I had had problems with this stuff before which did not have a happy ending.

Finally, after almost a mile, at a point where the path split into two, I found a suitable spot, and it even had a bench where we could sit and enjoy the evening sunshine. I dumped my pack and poles and immediately went back to help Rob, though he declined my offer to carry his rucksack for him, which is good because I don't think I would have been able to. We both collapsed onto the bench having walked around 22 miles, which for us city dwellers, was a very long way indeed.

The wind had died down completely, which made putting the tent up a doddle and having done so we enjoyed our nightly ritual of a coffee with a little something in it. The view from here was awesome, with Scarborough Castle and the north bay clearly visible to the south, and beyond that was Filey Brigg, our final and much sought-after finishing point. The sky was clear, and as the darkness came, stars twinkled on one by one. The temperature dropped accordingly with the clear sky, however, so it wasn't long before I rang Leeanne to let her know where we were and to make some arrangements for our pick up tomorrow, which I was told was already under control and sorted out.

After this, I just sat on the bench and watched the night darken around me as Rob had long since gone into the tent. A couple of walkers approached, and when they got to our little camp, a conversation began. Liz and Gail were avid walkers themselves, and had done the Coast to Coast as well as Hadrian's Wall, and were now section hiking the Cleveland Way. They said they were jealous of us being able to do it all at once, so I offered to show them my destroyed feet, an offer that you may be surprised to know was not taken up.

They were both on furlough from their jobs and had been making the most of the opportunity to be able to walk as much as possible, though family responsibilities meant no long walks such as ours. It turned out that Gail was from Driffield, a place that I had walked through on my last walk when I had decided, somewhat on the spur of the moment, to walk across the country in a straight line at a latitude of exactly, or as near as we could get anyway, of 54 degrees north. That had eventually turned into my first book, which sold surprisingly well and Rob had accompanied me on that walk too, as well as Chris, of course. As we had walked along, we found out about all sorts of hidden histories of people and places, some of which went into the book, some of which I told her now. That book ultimately led to this book.

Eventually, when it was almost properly dark, the ladies continued on their walk, and I went into the tent. The temperature had dropped considerably, and I climbed into my sleeping bag and zipped it up all around me as much as was possible, trying to keep my body warmth in. I lay awake for quite a while but drifted off at some point, waking for the first time just after midnight, when I nipped out of the tent to have a look at the night sky. It was still clear, and there was an almost full moon hovering over Scarborough Castle, with the town itself lit up and gently twinkling away, which was altogether an impressive sight. The gentle sound of the waves hitting the cliffs below us was very soothing, and when I got back in the tent, I was soon back in a deep sleep.

CHAPTER 7
Cloughton to Filey

The sun woke us up around 6 am, and we went through our usual routine of packing up and making a coffee almost without thinking about it. It had become our little ritual after these few days and was almost second nature. After covering around 91 miles in the last 5 days, both mine and Rob's feet were past their best, to say the least, and knees and ankles were feeling the strain too. The fact that we had covered an extra mile or so last night while looking for a campsite would hopefully make today a little bit easier, and we hoped to be finished for around 4 pm or so.

The weather today looked to be the best it had been so far, which meant that we could set off without waterproofs. Hopefully, this would mean that I would not find myself sweating after just a couple of miles, although my personal hygiene was already beyond anything that I could call nice, to be honest. We did have a blast of Rob's deodorant before we set off, quite a long one which half-emptied the can in fact, although I am not sure what help it was, to be honest.

The going was easy at first, a gentle downhill stroll in the early morning sunshine. We went through a small wood and then down and up one of those pointless dips that led us onto Cloughton Bay where we saw a couple of seals basking on the rocks below. Rounding this, we stopped for a quick rest at the top of a hill and had a sip of our coffee, before carrying on with much of the same for a few miles.

We passed a lookout point at Long Nab which had at one time been used for spotting enemy ships and planes. Two men sat inside with binoculars, and when we approached, they came out to chat. The hut was now used to spot migrating birds, they told us. I asked the taller one, who had been doing most of the talking, what was the most unusual thing he had seen, and he told me that he had once seen a lady do an interesting trick with a ping pong ball while he was on holiday, which was not really what I was getting at, but I must admit, it answered the question.

Moving on, the path zigged and zagged relentlessly, and Scarborough, and particularly the castle, were getting noticeably closer whenever we caught a glimpse of them. There were more people around too, many of them with their four-legged friends in tow, and one jogger flew past with her dog pulling her along at an impressive speed. This was probably not a very good idea, as this particular dog was an Afghan hound, and they are renowned for being one of the thickest dogs, apparently. I can independently confirm that this is not quite true, though, as that title actually belongs to my son's dog, which is a cross between a shih zhu and a poodle, and I affectionately call him our shitpoodle.

Rounding Scalby Ness, which offered a great view of the north bay, we descended down one last hill and hit Scarborough itself. A footbridge took us over Scalby Beck, which is where we joined the promenade of this lovely little seaside town.

Scalby Beck is interesting for one thing, it is partly fake. The River Derwent, which has its source just over the hill at Fylingdales, originally flowed to the sea around here, via what is now Esk Beck. It was a bit further to the south, though, and hit the sea at a place called Monkey Island. Monkey Island sadly never had monkeys and has anyway been washed away, but at the end of the ice age the river silted up and therefore made the River Derwent go on a 150-mile long diversion all the way around Yorkshire, rather than its original 4-mile course, which is, to be honest, a more interesting route surely.

The Derwent used to flood a lot, which annoyed the people in the area, so some local and presumably rich folks decided to play God with the landscape and created something called Sea

Cut, which saw the floodwaters from the Derwent take a short cut to the sea via here. One of the big boys on this project was a guy called George Caley; remember that name, as we will run into him later on.

Anyway, by now we had the Scarborough Sea Life Centre to our right, where you can go and see penguins and jellyfish if your heart so desires, though still no monkeys, and strangely, they had an on-site, pirate-themed crazy golf course. I had been here many years before, and distinctly remember one of my kids rather loudly telling me to look at the jellyfish's testicles.

Anyway, we did not so desire, so just carried on walking. Almost immediately, though, a plague of locusts descended upon us and began following us as we walked along. They were probably sand-flies, to be honest, but whatever they were, there were thousands of them. I wondered if it was the fact that we had been in the wilderness for so long and had become so smelly which had caused this, as no matter where we went, the flies followed. Luckily, after a half a mile or so, we walked out of the cloud, and into relative paradise. Beach huts adorned our right, and a small café looked promising but did not offer a full English, so we moved on.

Rob had decided to get the bus around the headland into the south bay as his foot was still hurting, but I said I would walk around and meet him there. He tried to persuade me to get on it as well on the premise that this bit was boring, dangerous, and/or haunted, but I was having none of it. I hadn't previously spent much time here, so I was sure I would enjoy the walk around. We had decided that we could probably get some breakfast around there as well, as there would be a wider choice of places to eat, but just before the bus stop, I spotted a decent looking café and decided to check out the menu. Breakfast was available, so we dumped our packs and grabbed a seat and waited for some service.

Very soon, a young man came out and offered to get us a menu, but I explained that we already knew what we wanted. I expected him to take our order, but he said it was bar service and directed me indoors. Nobody was wearing a facemask, but out of an abundance of caution, I put mine on, and then joined a queue to order our food. After five minutes, another customer mentioned that it was separate queues for food and drink, and of course, I was in the wrong one, so I jumped across. I ordered two breakfasts and two large cokes, and because of eat out to help out, this was half price, which was great. I paid by card and stood aside to wait for our drinks, but after just a moment, the lady that had served me called me over and told me that my card payment had failed. I tried again, but it did not work, but luckily, I had cash and paid with that. I think the problem was that I had tried to pay contactlessly, but every now and then the banks make you put your number in just for security reasons, but I never did really find out.

Everyone was looking at me, and I think they presumed I was living on the street due to my shoddy appearance and bank card problems, and I guess they were right, technically at least. Anyway, she gave me our drinks and said someone would bring the food out, so I went outside and sat in the sun with Rob. Looking around, although it was early, around 9.30 am, the place was bustling, particularly the cafes, and with the shining blue sea to my left, I felt like I could have been on holiday in the med. I told Rob he needed some suncream on today, as I watched his big shiny head sizzle in the strong sunshine in a manner that our bacon was simultaneously experiencing somewhere behind us, and I borrowed a bit myself.

I had last been here maybe two or three years ago, funnily enough with Rob, but also with both of our wives. We had come to see a Lionel Richie concert at the nearby open-air theatre, and I remembered that we had been very lucky with the weather that night. It was a beautiful summers evening, with a clear blue sky all around that slowly turned deeper and deeper until it became totally black. I also remember that it was Richie's birthday, which was a bit embarrassing as we didn't even bring a card, but I think he was just happy we had popped by to see him and had given him £50 for our tickets.

If you are of a certain age, and if you ever

come here, you might just recognize the theatre. It is very distinctive, set in a natural amphitheatre, a tricky word to spell if ever there was one, with the stage on an island in the middle of a lake. This was, you see, the home of a crazy television show throughout the 1980s called *It's a Knockout*, which involved teams of people dressing up in ridiculously clumsy costumes and racing around obstacle courses and generally knocking the living daylights out of each other. Unfortunately, the presenter of the show, Stuart Hall, a well-known figure in British TV, spent much of the 1980s and presumably much of his time on this show, grooming underage girls and has since been both prosecuted and disgraced.

My thoughts were interrupted as breakfast arrived, and I devoured mine in double-quick time. I could have eaten another one given the chance but decided not to have anything else as we would be meeting the ladies later that day when they picked us up, and we had promised them food in return. We sat for a while after finishing our breakfasts as we felt there was no rush whatsoever today and just enjoyed the fresh air and the sunshine for a change. Eventually, though, we had to move, and we had both become a bit stiff since sitting down around an hour before.

As Rob hobbled away to the bus stop in front of us, he appeared to be struggling considerably, so maybe the bus ride would do him good and give him a while to rest at the other end while he waited for me to catch him up. I managed to walk around a quarter of a mile before his bus passed me, and laughed as he gave me the royal wave, which was better than the bird, I thought. I noticed he was wearing a face mask on the bus, which was compulsory of course, although as I never really use buses, I had not particularly thought about it. If I go anywhere, I tend to either walk or cycle, or if I really have to, I will use my car. Although my car is electric, and therefore better for the local environment, it is more about health and exercise that encourages me to walk or use my bike, and I try to walk at least ten miles a day on most days, which sounds a lot but isn't.

It was a pleasant walk around the north bay, and most people said good morning or hello as I tramped along. Joggers and cyclists all happily shared the same path, which was very wide at this point, and some people had been camping out next to the skate park. They were only now beginning to come out of their tents, where I saw them having a good stretch and yawning lazily. The air was clean and fresh, and in its early days as a resort, many people came here for exactly that reason. Amazingly, at that time, one of the treatments suggested to treat tuberculosis was simply a trip to the seaside and all that it entailed. Anne Bronte, one of the famous Bronte sisters, who was suffering from tuberculosis, came here to avail herself of this famous sea air cure on the 24th May 1849. On the 28th May, she died. Just saying.

Dunkings in the sea were also common, not quite as you would a witch, but not far off. Another way to think about it is waterboarding, that now well-known modern method of torture. The idea was that the continuous shock to your body would get your adrenaline pumping, and when you were almost dead, you would get a good massage to get your circulation, and possibly heart, going again, followed by that good old British favourite, a cup of tea. Sometimes you would be prescribed a drink of the stuff too, and I am on about seawater here, not tea. If you were lucky, you would get a bit of honey in it, although I am not sure that this would have been enough, to be honest, and if you were British, you might even want milk in your seawater. We put milk in everything, us Brits, to the disgust of foreigners everywhere, even our tea. Seawater was even prescribed to treat leprosy. Every morning, a patient would be instructed to drink a pint of England's finest salty stuff, and after nine months or so, leprosy would no longer be an issue. The patient was dead, but the leprosy was no longer a problem. Seriously, if you drink seawater, you will eventually die of dehydration. As proof of this, all Victorians are dead. Don't do it.

As I rounded the headland, there was a sign of what was to come, though I did not realize this at the time. A large family of maybe around two dozen people were congregating across the whole path, talking animatedly and making liberal use of swear words. I'm no prude and quite often make use of expletives myself, but these people had it down to a fine art. Even the kids were having a go, and when a wasp chased one of the young ladies, and I'm being generous by using the word ladies here, every other word began first with an F, then a B and finally, and even I don't use this word, several beginning with a C.

I tried to move past them, but they seemed to flow along with me, but every cloud has a silver lining. One of the young scallywags, who had been annoying me by repeatedly getting in front of me no matter which way I went, tripped over, went down, and did an impressive skid several feet along the promenade using his face, which must have really hurt. At this, the whole group stopped while they scraped up what was left of him, and I made my escape.

Unfortunately, I made my escape into the south bay of Scarborough, which is, shall we say, the chavvy side. Apparently, Scarborough is Britain's oldest seaside resort and people have been coming here since the 1650s, believe it or not. I had read that the town gets 1.5 million visitors every year, and by the looks of it, most of them had decided to drop by today. Anyone who knows me might know that I am not a great fan of seaside places that target the, well, there is no other way to say this, target the budget market. Don't misread this, I like Scarborough very much, it is a very nice place that I have been to very often over the years and has retained some qualities that many other seaside places have long ago lost. And indeed, I usually find myself at the budget end of, well, everything. But in all honesty, you can keep this bit. Amusement arcades and chip shops are great in the right measure, but this was just too much for me, and I just wanted to plough through it as quickly as possible.

There is a lot to be said for Scarborough, though. It is the birthplace of none other than George Caley, who if you remember, diverted a river a while back. He is better known as the first proper aeronautical engineer though, and some go so far as calling him the *Father of Aeronautics*. He built a glider which managed to achieve flight way back in 1853, almost 50 years to the day before the Wright brothers first flew, although he used his footman John Appleby as his reluctant test pilot just in case, the chicken.

The town also gave to the world Sir Ben Kingsley, a most excellent actor, though his original name was Krishna Pandit Bhanji. He changed it because he thought this would help progress his career. Unfortunately, Scarborough also managed to belch out notorious sexual predator and general weirdo Jimmy Saville, though we can't blame the town for that, of course. Like Stuart Hall, though, Saville managed to get away with his despicable crimes for so long because he was classed as untouchable. That both have strong links to Scarborough as well as the BBC makes me wonder if they knew each other well. On a more positive note, sort of, the town also gave us Thomas Harland, who went on to form the Harland and Wolff shipyard that built the unsinkable ship Titanic, of course, which as we all know, promptly sank almost as soon as it got wet.

The town itself was famously attacked by the German Navy in December 1914 and became the first place that civilians have been injured on the British mainland during the First World War. The attack was so shocking that *Remember Scarborough* became a rallying cry for the rest of the war. Over 500 shells fell in less than 20 minutes, resulting in severe damage to the town and the deaths of 19 people. The Germans then moved on to attack Whitby followed by a further, more intense attack on Hartlepool. Although there were more casualties in Hartlepool, it was the deaths of civilians in Scarborough that really resonated with the nation and imposed a sense of shock and disgust at the ungentlemanly nature of this kind of warfare. As an example of this, the last person to be killed was a young boy called George Taylor, who was, in fact, the only boy scout to be dispatched in the war. He had just popped out to buy a newspaper and was a victim of being in the wrong place at the wrong time. This was never forgotten, though, as the Brits eventually got the Germans back in the Second World War and the first bomb that they dropped on Berlin hit an elephant. As unlikely as that sounds, it's true. Why, oh why, do they not teach us this stuff in school?

I finally met up with Rob near the harbour where he had commandeered a bench, so I sat down and joined him for a quick rest. We were running low on water, and while I had been walking around the bay, he had been on a mission to restock, and he decanted some of what he had into my camel pack, as we figured we would not need a full one each. This done, we got up to go, but I was stopped in my tracks by what I saw next. Rob must have noticed because he saw my gaping mouth hanging wide open, and asked me what on earth was wrong.

I explained to Rob that the guy walking past us right at that very moment was an absolute spitting image of my uncle Raymond. The absolute double. Not kind of looked like him but exactly looked like him, even down to the clothes he wore. Rob looked puzzled and suggested maybe it was my uncle Raymond and that rather than standing there gaping at him like an idiot, which the poor guy had by now noticed and had a somewhat worrisome look on his face, I should perhaps go and say hello and see if it was him. I then had to explain to Rob that I had last seen Raymond around ten years earlier and that this last sighting was at his funeral, so I suspected, quite strongly in fact, indeed hoped, that this guy before me now was not Raymond from Hull after all, but nonetheless, the likeness was uncanny. It didn't matter now anyway, because by now the man, whoever he was but certainly not Raymond from Hull, was running up the promenade away from me as fast as he could go. He was moving impressively quickly too, with the occasional alarming glance backwards to see if he was being followed by a gaping-mouthed weirdo.

Drama over, we stumbled on southwards, veering left and right to avoid overweight people of various types stuffing their faces with chips, sticks of rock and candy floss, sometimes all at the same time, an impressive feat if ever I saw one. Most of them wore clothing that was too tight for them, or that revealed a midriff that was probably only appropriate for after the nine o'clock watershed. Like I said earlier, I'm not a prude, and each to their own, but I appreciate that people do not probably want or need to look at various bits of my flibby flabby anatomy, particularly not at this early hour or at any hour at all for that matter, and I would sometimes appreciate the same courtesy, particularly after I have not long ago had a full English breakfast. So, unless you want to see that breakfast make a come-back, please keep your junk in the trunk. Thank you.

We passed a big wheel, which seem to be all the rage nowadays, and I wondered what you would be able to see from the top of it. Denmark maybe? Probably not. There was a high hill to the other side, so I guessed not much really. Maybe a nice view of the promenade? I went to have a look but at £5 a go, I decided that I would probably get as good a view when we went up the hill. You might think that I am a grumpy old sourpuss now, and indeed I am, bah humbug. Anyway, the sign said that the ride took you 35 metres up in the air for ten minutes and was the perfect family day out. Hold on, a day out lasting ten minutes? But wait, there is more. Immediately next to, and presumably part of this attraction, was Captain Jack's adventure golf, a mini-golf game that I prefer to call crazy golf. It was once again pirate-themed, aarg, and the instructions for play started with the word *ahoy*, so I'm in anyway, or at least I was until I found out that they wanted another £5 for the pleasure. Bah humbug.

    The mini-golf reminded me of a Bob Hoskins film I had seen long ago, which was filmed back at Whitby, and also called Captain Jack. Later on, I would learn that this film was loosely based on true events, though at the time I presumed that the story was so outlandish, it must have been made up. It involved William Scoresby, sort of, but was centred on the actions of a guy called Jack Lammiman. Lammiman, who ran his pleasure boat out of Whitby, came up with a hare-brained scheme to sail up to the Arctic Circle so he could lay a plaque in memory of William Scoresby the younger, and if you were paying attention earlier you would know exactly who I mean. The authorities got wind of it and used every trick in the book to stop him doing this, ultimately impounding his ship. Lammiman had other ideas, however, and managed to gather together a motley crew of old-age pensioners, a retired policeman and a parson. After building a crow's nest on the top of his boat in tribute to Scoresby senior, he finally set sail, sneaking out of Whitby harbour under cover of the local fishing fleet. A massive search ensued involving the navy and the coast guard, but all to no avail. Jack got his trip, and was greeted with a hero's welcome upon his return to Whitby. Several weeks later, however, he found himself up in court and thrown in prison. I think he had the last laugh though, managing to make a tidy sum when the film was made.

Wandering a bit further on, we were almost near to where the shops and amusements ended but decided to make use of the facilities before we left the town, not knowing if or when we would find another toilet. Rob went first, and I sat on some steps beside a small shop and waited, keeping an eye on our rucksacks which we had put down near to a fence just a few feet away. A lady came up to me and offered me a ten-pound note, which I thought odd, as this doesn't happen very often, or ever, come to think of it. She had mistaken me for the stallholder, and if I had had my wits about me, I could have made a fair bit of money. As it was, I told her that it wasn't my stall, and was surprised to note that this made her a bit annoyed, giving me a bit of a humph as she turned away.

Once we got going again, the climb up

started immediately, and we made our way to the top of the cliff where the path once again took the high route. At least the path was nice, which helped, though towards the top the incline became crazy steep, and I found myself inching along very slowly. A man on his way down took one look at my backpack and laughed, and a lady passed shortly after with her daughter and asked if I needed an ambulance perhaps, or maybe a nice coffin.

At the top, though, there was a fine selection of benches to crawl towards and quietly pass away on as well, if necessary. I dropped my pack and waited for Rob, and when he turned up, he had beads of sweat dripping down his now shiny red forehead. I dug some Kendal Mint Cake out, hoping to get the energy required that would help us finish this thing, and after a substantial glug of water, we trundled on. A couple came up to us and asked us how we were doing. They were out walking their dog, which was busy retrieving a stick which he then brought back. Rob took the opportunity to throw the stick, which unfortunately disappeared over a very steep hill into some nettles, and I had visions of the dog jumping to its prickly end. Luckily it wasn't that stupid and managed to make its way down carefully to reclaim what was probably his favourite toy. The lady asked us if we had encountered any problems with flies on the North Beach, which confirmed that the problem was not solely us and our hygiene.

The path took us towards, and then through, a caravan park that was buzzing with life although full of kids. We got talking to a family from Middlesbrough who were out doing a circular walk themselves, and when we told them how far we had walked, their jaws dropped. We walked along with them for a while, but then pressed ahead as their pace was a little too slow. I guess when you are out walking with a purpose, like us, then you walk faster than when you are just rambling on.

We came across a dip where the path took us down a couple of dozen steps in a haphazard and worrying manner, with a narrow path that would make social distancing impossible. A couple coming up the same path kindly inserted themselves into some thorns, which looked painful, but in that British way, the man apologised to us for the pain he had caused himself and the blood he had dripped on the path and how sorry he was and all that. Us Brits tend to say sorry for a lot of things that don't really warrant an apology, but we are certainly not the worst offenders. That would be the Canadians, eh. The government there even went so far as to pass a law in 2009 that stipulated an apology in itself was not to be treated as an admission of guilt in a court of law. Amazing. This is the same country that is not even sure when it became a sovereign state, with its Supreme Court ruling somewhat vaguely that it probably happened sometime between 1919 and

1931.

Anyway, he was called Jim, his wife Maureen and their little dog was Banjo, and after we enticed him to come out of the bush by assuring him that we didn't bite unless provoked or cornered, we struck up a conversation. He told us that he lived locally and that we would have big problems with the path for the next couple of miles. As he talked, his little dog was yapping at my leg as if it was a nice piece of steak, or so I thought.

Jim advised us to divert from the Cleveland Way and take the next left down to the beach instead. We should then walk along to the headland, go straight over that and on into Cayton Bay, and rejoin the actual path at Lucy's Café, which also made a fine selection of burgers, hot-dogs and drinks, apparently. He exuded confidence and was very well-spoken, so we thought what the hell, we'll follow the directions of a complete stranger. I suspected he was ex-military judging by the way he gave us the tide times, with low tide being at ten hundred hours, which was good to know. Banjo was now humping my leg, so I kicked him off as forcefully as I could without actually sending him over the cliff, and we moved on.

Following Jim's instructions, we found ourselves almost at the beach. Almost, however, in this case, means not on the beach at all, but we had come down such a very long way and had invested so much effort that we did not want to have to climb back up, so what was a 20-foot sheer cliff to get in our way. I encouraged Robin to go first, at least that way, I would have a soft landing when I also slipped and fell, landing on his dead, lifeless corpse. Somehow, we both managed to get down to the sand without any kind of life-threatening incident, which was a pleasant surprise, and we were busy congratulating ourselves on our new found mountaineering skills when we both went arse over tit on the seaweed. Luckily, no-one at all saw what happened apart from the dozen or so people who now stood laughing at us from the sand, but fear not, we carried on, using our sticks to balance us until we too made it to the safety of the sand.

We were in Cornelian Bay but did not yet know it as we slunk along the soft sand at a snail's pace. Ahead of us, we could see a couple of bunkers from the Second World War, which were now well past their best, and an older couple were scouring the beach looking for something or other. She was prodding the sand and carrying a bright red bag, and he was on his hands and knees digging some sort of hole. As we passed, I asked him if he was looking for something for lunch, perhaps, but he laughed and stood up to talk to us.

He was looking for cornelian, and it was he that told us the name of the beach and bay. Cornelian, he told us, was a reddish semi-precious gemstone relatively common on this beach, hence the name. He went on to tell us that Cornelian, similar to Sard, whatever the heck that was, had been used throughout antiquity by ancient civilizations including the Romans to make engraved gems for signet rings. It was also used by the Minoans and the Egyptians for various things and was really quite a handy thing to find lying around for free, and he told us that he and his wife liked to make arrow-heads out of it for the grand-kids. I'm kidding, they make jewellery really, I just wanted to see if you are still paying attention.

He went on to ask us if we had been to Skinningrove; we had, we excitedly told him, and he said that at the far end of that beach you can find perfectly spherical iron balls, which had been washed around here and there to make them round. I was amazed by all this knowledge and asked him if he was a geologist, and he said no, he was a butcher.

As we walked off, I found myself looking at the ground for some cornelian, and managed to find a few bits that looked suspiciously like the description that he had just given me. I also found a massive lump of rock and offered it to Rob as a souvenir to keep from our trip, but he declined, the ungrateful curmudgeon.

Reaching the end of this beach, we passed the second bunker and had a little tiff about whether or not it had fallen down from above at some point, as a result of the beach eroding over the years. Rob reckoned it had, but I thought it had been built where it still was, my reasoning being that if you stuck a machine gun out of the slits, you could efficiently mow down everyone on that beach within a matter of seconds, with very little risk to yourself. Of course, you might have to do a few years in prison if you tried this, but that's not the point.

Beyond was a slick and steep slope made of freshly moistened mud. I went first, only for the reason that if Rob fell, scratch that, when Rob fell, I didn't want him taking me out on the way down. It was a slow and careful splodge up to the top, but getting up there revealed the vast expanse of sand that was Cayton Bay in all its might and was a welcome sight. The path down to the beach was almost as bad as the one we had just come up, and I'm not even sure the word path applies here. A couple of false alerts later, when I thought that my rate of descent was going to speed up considerably, and possibly fatally, I put my right foot on the ground and breathed a sigh of relief. It wasn't over yet though; more seaweed and slippery rocks stood between us and the sand, which necessitated a careful and slow negotiation. When I finally reached the bottom, I stopped to rest and waited for Rob.

It was now a straightforward walk to the slipway in the distance, and as we went on, the density of the people increased significantly. I reckoned there were several hundred people on the beach, which was fine as it was so large, but they all seemed to be congregating in one place, close to the slipway. I had seen pictures in the papers about overcrowded seaside resorts, but seeing it in person was something else altogether.

We ploughed straight through the crowds, up the slipway past Lucy's, and found a bench to sit on. Rob went to see Lucy and to grab us both a drink and came back with two ice-cold cans which went down a treat. As we sat there, a cool looking buff guy went past in a full wet suit and carrying a surfboard, and I thought to myself that he was why girls went to the beach. Luckily, the reason that boys went to the beach also walked past a minute later, so we stayed a while.

It was no surprise that the path carried on up a steep hill to a car park at the top. A nice car with a private number plate that more or less spelt out Cayton was parked here, and judging by the number of cars parked all around here, the owner of this vehicle must also have been the owner of the car park and all of the profits that it brought in.

The path took us around Yons Nab, a small headland pointing north, though I did not know what it was called at the time. I only looked it up later as there is an impressive pillar here, which looks as if it might be collapsing at some point shortly and would be a spectacular sight when it does.

The path then took us along a route which edged behind some holiday chalets nicely between them and the cliff. Much of it was overgrown but every now and then a small patch of it was perfectly manicured, presumably by the occupant. One man was out cutting his grass and was taking great care to ensure that he didn't cut any of his neighbour's grass in the process. He had meticulously marked out some wooden stakes and strung some string in between them to mark his border, and it was this point that he was cutting up to and no further.

I jokingly asked him how far he was going, Scarborough perhaps, and he looked at me with a straight face and said up to the line. I gave him my best *okay* grin and moved on. Unfortunately, I chose to move on in the wrong direction, which took me up a steep hill and into a field that seemed to be a dead end. I sat on the bench and waited for Rob to get to the top before I told him that we had come the wrong way. I suppose I could have waved and shouted to him not to follow me up there, but that would have been no fun at all and he would have missed out on a great view. A man sat on the next bench holding some binoculars confirmed our mistake, saying that it would add miles if we continued on in this direction. He said he was watching the whales off-shore and had seen a couple already, as well as some dolphins. After a brief rest, we headed downhill once more.

Just behind this holiday park, somewhere hidden away, is the Scarborough Fair Collection of old rides and vintage vehicles. My parents told me about it, and I was a bit sceptical until I actually paid it a visit. It has all of the old favourites including carousels, steam engines, and organs, including a Granada Mansfield Wurlitzer which shared a stage with the Beatles, my dad's favourite band. I wasn't willing to go up the hill for that today, and besides, I was told it was closed at the moment due to the pandemic, like so many attractions and businesses. If you get the chance though, you should go.

Before we move on, I have to mention the song of the same name which most people think was written by rock gods Simon and Garfunkel. The song I am on about may be obvious to some of you oldies, but if not, it's also called Scarborough Fair. If you have never heard this song, then I strongly urge you to listen to it, as it's both beautiful and haunting at the same time. I didn't understand what it was about for a good few years, so to save you some time, here is the plot. A guy is basically asking you to tell his former lover to go through a series of impossible tasks, such as making a seamless shirt and then washing it in a dry well, before he will take her back. This suggests she must have done something really, really bad, because when you actually think about it, both of these tasks would be tricky, to say the least.

He is asking you this on the assumption that you are going to Scarborough Fair where she can be found, although fair in this sense means something more like a market. In return, she then insists that he also complete some impossible tasks, and she will only complete her tasks when he has finished his. This is beginning to sound a bit like my wife, to be honest, and it also says that she maybe doesn't want him back.

Surprisingly, as previously hinted at, this song was not actually written by Simon and Garfunkel, and you may be astonished to learn that it is, in fact, hundreds of years old and was written in medieval times. Who knew? There are lots of theories surrounding its origins, but we will never know for sure, though my favourite is that the song is grounded in witchcraft, as the four herbs mentioned in the song – parsley, sage, rosemary and thyme – were actually ingredients for a medieval love potion.

Scarborough Fair did indeed exist, running for around six weeks every summer between the 13th and the 17th centuries, and there is some suggestion that the song may actually have been about the Black Death that swept across Europe during this time, with the herbs being the ingredients of something called Four Thieves Vinegar, which was thought to ward off the plague. In a way, I think it is actually kind of cool that this will forever remain a mystery, as it only adds to the story because if we knew the actual truth, it wouldn't be half as interesting.

Leaving the caravan parks behind, the path ahead looked flat and easy, and I figured we were almost finished. Filey Brigg kept tantalizingly showing itself to us, so it was just a case of head down and move on. There were not that many people around, just the occasional walker, but we did bump into a French couple every now and then who were both very sweet and quite obviously in love. They'll learn, I thought. Now living in York on their gap year, which was plagued by tourists they said ironically, they had come here for some peace and quiet. They had chosen well because there was no one else around. We told them that we should have been in France this week along with our families, to which they commented that Yorkshire was just as beautiful, if not more so, but with a less sexy accent. They were correct, of course. Many people do not appreciate what they have got on their own doorstep, and this year has seen the rise of the staycation, where people choose to holiday at home. The UK has a whole multitude of habitats, environments and landscapes far beyond what any other country of a similar size has, and can beat off some much larger countries too. It is, possibly, a continent unto itself, although one in miniature. Plus, if you fancy a laugh, you can go to the seaside on any given weekend where you will see some right sights, which is probably down to a distinct lack of style, and possibly self-awareness, by quite a lot of people, and we all really do have funny accents.

I kept having to stop for Rob, who was now going very slowly due to all of his injuries. I did not mind, of course, as it is usually the other way around. I wanted us to reach the end together, but I could not have walked at the speed he was currently moving at as it was just not my natural walking speed. As I waited, I thought I saw a couple of dolphins in the waters below, and this was confirmed a few seconds later as they both jumped out of the water, which was a splendid sight. And if you fancy a shag, this is also the place to come. They live along the cliffs here, along with cormorants and the odd puffin, though there are not as many as can be found at nearby Bempton.

I reached what was possibly the edge of Filey, so I stopped to wait for him one more time, and I spent a few minutes looking out over the town. It was bigger than I thought, and I could quite clearly see the spire of the church. I had read that it had been damaged in the Great Earthquake of 1931 but had quickly been fixed. In the same article, someone had described that rather underwhelming event as something similar to the noise a radiator makes, or perhaps a cat falling off a wardrobe. To me, though, those two events would surely sound completely different. I reckoned a cat falling off a wardrobe would be quite a high-pitched noise followed by a thud followed by a laugh, mine. My cat once fell off the back of the telly late one night, just as I was just dozing off, and it scared the living daylights out of me. I don't mind cats, but I have said before that they are a bit pointless as a pet, but we should be lucky we have them. Way back in the 1400s, Pope Gregory IX declared war on them and said that they were agents of the devil. I can see where he is coming from, because my cat often tries to nick my toast. He only waged war on black cats though, I mean, he wasn't a complete lunatic or anything.

     Anyway, what else has Filey given us? Well, Tony Blair's dad, Leo, which was fine, but this also and obviously started the chain of events that led to, well, Tony Blair. Hmmm. I'll let you decide. Anyway, Leo Blair was originally born Charles Parsons. He was the illegitimate son of two travelling entertainers and was later adopted, by the Blair's obviously, and did very well for himself, studying law and becoming a barrister and later a lecturer. His natural parents did try to get him back at a later date but were unsuccessful. Strange how things work out.

     Billy Butlin built (that's a mouthful) one of his first holiday camps here, which was a great idea, but he started building it in 1939, which was not. After the war, however, it opened fully, and it was a big draw for holidaymakers for years to come. Now long gone, the site has since been turned into a massive housing development, presumably by a dyslexic builder, who decided to call it The Bay Filey. Billy himself was an interesting character, and he used to carry a cut-throat razor around with him all the time, just in case he bumped into one of the many enemies he had made. Described by some as a rogue, a charmer and a ladies' man, and by his own nephew as a gangster, he did give a lot of money to charities and helped kick start the careers of the likes of

Benny Hill and Cliff Richard. So, there you go.

After what seemed like aeons, Rob caught me up, and we finally caught sight of the finishing post. We walked up to it together and unceremoniously but simultaneously plonked ourselves down, absolutely shattered and utterly beaten. We just sat there in silence for a while and never even bothered to take a photo, but chatted quietly together about how much we had enjoyed this walk, but oh, how glad we were that it was all over. We shook hands and congratulated each other, and as simple as that, we were done.

And then we talked about the next one.

CHAPTER 8
Conclusion

The ladies arrived to pick us up and may have commented extensively about both our cave-dweller type appearance and our somewhat spicy aroma. My wife kindly and thoughtfully told me that I smelled like a wet horse. We politely reminded them that we had effectively been living in a field for the last six days so it was tough and they should deal with it. Truth be told, it was borderline as to whether or not they were going to make us walk home, so we finished off the can of deodorant between us and kept the car windows open for the journey back.

I think that Rob and I had both had enough of walking, at least for the time being, and our thirst for it had been momentarily quenched, for various reasons. Blisters had been a problem for me, at least, to the point of making walking difficult. One of my blisters had started to heal, only for another one to begin forming underneath almost immediately, which is not something I had encountered before, and I put it down partly to the fact that I had not worn my shoes in sufficiently beforehand. Lesson learned I assured myself, hoping for better things next time. Rob had nearly toppled over a couple of times, as had I, and had it not been for our hiking poles, it could have ended badly for either of us. The shoes themselves had performed really well. They never caught fire or fell off, for instance, which is always a plus, but on a serious note, they had kept my feet dry, even through some fairly heavy showers, which is essential when walking any distance for days on end. My muscles ached, but a persistent problem that I had been having with the back of my left ankle seemed to have eased off a bit, which I put down to using shoes rather than boots. The solar panel was a good idea, but proved problematic when charging phones directly, and needed continuous bright sunlight. It seemed to work better with small USB chargers and managed to charge them even in cloudy conditions. Paradoxically, although the sun had not had the power to charge a phone, both Rob and I had been sunburned on that last day. Despite all of this, though, we both agreed that we had really enjoyed this walk, but we also both agreed that it would have been better if Chris had come too, so maybe next time.

    I had also decided that I had brought too many items of clothing, and that next time I would be able to lighten my load a bit, as well as not bringing so much food. There really is no point in carrying such things around in tiny little England. Next time, I would be brutal. Anyway, if I did run out of food, I figured I could do to shed a few pounds. When I jumped on the scales back at home, I was quite surprised to find that I had lost a little bit of weight, and Rob said that he had too. Walking is, therefore, in my opinion, an easy exercise for almost anybody who can put one foot in front of another. It doesn't put too much stress on either your joints or your heart, and I always tell everyone that the further you walk, the further you will be able to walk and the further you will want to walk. And the best thing of all is that it is free. No gym memberships, no specialist equipment needed, nothing. I am very much into a habit of walking nowadays, and I found that when I got one of those step counter type smartwatches a while back, I increased my activity by quite a bit, which is both interesting to know and a good tip to pass on.

And of course, if you walk enough, you will eventually lose a bit of weight and get a bit fitter, with every step you take requiring the use of around 200 muscles. If you walk for an hour or so a day, you will burn at least a couple of hundred calories or thereabouts, and by the end of the week, this could be a couple of thousand, which is a couple of bottles of wine for your efforts. If you really don't want to walk, then I'm told that banging your head against a wall for an hour burns around 150 calories, which is, however, somewhat less than an hour of sex, at around 400, as well as not being quite as much fun. Take your pick, or even combine the two. The world is your oyster. Just don't do it while walking. And here's a thought for you - the average person walks the equivalent of five times around the world in their lifetime, which is just mad when you think about it. Oh and one last thing, don't post your fitness regime to social media, doubly so if you're combining headbanging with the other banging. People who do so are more likely to suffer from psychological problems. Seriously. You heard it here first.

A few days after we got home, and after my body had had the chance to start to get back to normal, I received a call one morning from the test and trace people, who told me that I had signed a register at a café in Scarborough a few days earlier. Indeed I had, I thought, immediately worried. It turns out that someone who was also present at around the same time as myself had subsequently tested positive for Coronavirus. I must admit that I was a little alarmed and immediately went to live in the man cave at the bottom of my garden until I got the all-clear. My son is immune-compromised following a solid organ transplant a couple of years before and had spent most of the year under intense and strict lockdown. We had also taken extra precautions, certainly more than most, in order to protect him, which I think perplexed some people around us and I figured that they just did not understand the additional risks faced by vulnerable people.

Luckily, I got a test pretty quickly. This was just before something seems to have gone drastically wrong with the testing system that would then result in people having to travel many miles for a test, which dominated the news for quite some time. I had my result within around 48 hours though, and it was thankfully negative, of course, so I was able to breathe a huge sigh of relief. But this brought home the reality of things around us at this very odd time.

I suspect, therefore, that it might be quite some time before we get out to do another long walk. Winter is fast approaching, and with it, the cloud that is the pandemic, on top of the normal flu and cold season. People will spend more time indoors and increase the risk of transmission, so it is quite likely at some point that our liberties will once again be restricted by the powers that be, and whatever your opinions are on the necessity of this, I think we can all agree that it is annoying.

On a final note, we had spent much of our time lost on this walk, but not necessarily lost in the sense of not knowing where we were. In this sense, lost means distracted from the stresses and strains of everyday life, or to put it another way, lost in the walk itself.

So, if you are reading this at a time when you are able and free to go out there and explore and enjoy the world around you, then might I suggest that you put down this book straight away, and go and do exactly that, and get lost in the walk.

I hope you have enjoyed reading this book, which is my second that has been published. What seems like a very long time ago, in a world untouched by lockdowns and viruses, I walked across England at a latitude of 54 Degrees North, and wrote about what I found out along the way. Please feel free to have a look at this book which is simply called *54 Degrees North*, and there is a bit more information on the next page.

Although the world has changed considerably since then, I hope I have demonstrated that it is not impossible to get out there and go do something extraordinary. I never would have thought that I would have been capable of either walking such distances or of writing and publishing a book, and certainly not of combining the two. I know it might not be much in the scheme of things, but it means such a lot to me.

I plan to continue to do this as long as I can, and therefore have a small request. Writers make their living when people become aware of their work, and for a newbie like me, it is difficult to become established. Therefore, if you are able to share knowledge of my work on platforms such as Facebook or Instagram, I would be very grateful. Reviews also help others make a choice on whether to buy books as well, so if you have enjoyed this book, please bear this in mind. Thank you for reading, now get your shoes on and get out there!

BOOKS BY THIS AUTHOR

54 Degrees North

Drawing a straight line across England at a latitude of exactly 54 degrees and walking along it as close as he can, join Paul Amess as he sets out to learn about this tiny strip of the country and its history including events, people and places. Starting on the east coast in Yorkshire, and somehow ending up in Lancashire, he encounters murders, film stars, witches and more, all linked in more ways than you might imagine.

Discover what links York with Lancaster, and what an alien has to do with Victorian bridges. Learn about the blind man that built many of our roads and the boffins at Aldermaston that wanted to drop a nuclear bomb on them. This is a ramble across our beloved little island that unearths all sorts of unexpected tales and weaves them together in a narrative like no other.

Coast To Coast: Finding Wainwright's England

Join Paul as he follows in the great Alfred Wainwright's footsteps on one of the world's best known and most popular walks. Taking in beautiful valleys, misty moors, lovely lakes and pleasing plains, find about about the literal and spiritual highs and lows of this 192 mile walk from St Bees to Robin Hood's Bay, all told in a flowing, candid and light-hearted story.Delving into the history as he goes along, this book will make you want to follow in his footsteps yourself, or if you have already done the Coast to Coast, you will want to grab your shoes and do it again.Mysterious monsters, funny facts and famous figures await.

Who knew that there could be so much history attached to this walk. Bridges built for lovers, amazing stories of pirates, devastating murders, stone circles, plots to blow the lake district sky high and ghost stories are all amusingly told against the backdrop of the walk itself.Paul and his friends spend two weeks tracing Wainwrights footsteps in search of an England of old, one that may not have changed as much as you would expect. Faced with challenges from the weather, from themselves and from other hikers, they get drenched, sunbuned and lost, all in equal proportions, and time and again are forced to hide in pubs.Will they make it? Read on to find out . . . .

Printed in Great Britain
by Amazon